THE
MOTHERS-IN-LAW

THE
MOTHERS-IN-LAW

Leola Sanders Huey

C.L.I.P.
Creative Unity Publishing

The Mothers-In-Law

ISBN 978-0-9822796-9-4

Cover Design: Donna Osborn Clark at CreationsByDonna@gmail.com

Layout and Interior Design: www.CreationByDonna.com

Editing: Timothy G. Green at Inkaissance: inkaissance@gmail.com

Published by: Creative Unity Publishing
www.CreativeUnityPublishing.net

Book is printed in 16 point font size which is the standard for Large Print.
Text Font used: Tiresias LPfont part of the Tiresias™ family of font.
For large print publications.
Copyright 2000, 2003 The Royal National Institute for the Blind

Scripture quotations used in this book are from
THE HOLY BIBLE, King James Version

Manufactured in the United States of America

First Edition

Acknowledgments

I would like to thank the following people for their help in bringing this book to completion. Without your help it would not exist.

I want to thank Kacie Hankins, an eighteen year old high school student, who helped me to edit this book. Can you see an eighteen year old working with an 88 year old senior? Neither could my daughter. She said that I must take pictures of us. Kacie patiently worked with me in editing this book. Never let it be said that young people have no time for old folks. Without her kind patience towards me you would not be reading this book.

I also want to give a hardy thank you to Renee Hankins, Kacie's mother, a teacher who proofread the manuscript.

And of course I want to thank my son in law and daughter for reading my first draft and giving me valuable advice that enhanced the book.

Thanks to Adrien Love for bringing her computer expertise to help me correct any computer problems that I came across.

A shout out and a hardy thank you goes to Donna at Creation By Donna and C.U.P. Creative Unity Publishing for publishing my book. I know it will be a number one seller with your expertise because you almost made my first book, *Oneda*, a number one seller with the cover you designed for it.

Preface

If you are a young person, have you ever wondered what it is like to be old? Are you afraid of getting old and sick with no one to help you? I hope these two questions will be answered for you after reading this book. I have tried to make this book reader friendly in responding to these two questions.

To give you a general idea, I began this book with a short script of two elderly mothers who are living in the same house and are cared for by their married children. To allay your fears of getting aged and dependent, I have written a compilation concerning people that I know who are advanced in age, yet successfully living alone and independently living.

I have also provided vital information for those in need of help to encourage them that these resources will support them in knowing that they do not have to face these fears alone. I have created this book to alleviate the myth of "*being old and useless*" after you reach a certain age.

God loves old folks and they never get too old for Him to use them according to His purpose.

Abraham was 75 years old when He called him to make a nation from his seed and 100 years old when Sarah, his wife, gave birth to their son of promise at the age of 90.

Moses was 80 years old and Aaron, his brother, was 83 years old when God called them to deliver His children from Egypt. So please know that you are never too old and useless; don't believe it at all!

Note to readers:

The names of the characters in this book have been changed to protect their privacy and identity.

The title of this book was given as such because one of the mothers was asked if they were related. "Yes." said the oldest one. "We are Mothers in law." So meet... the Mothers in Law.

Table of Contents

Part
1

Introduction

This short script is about two aging parents who are cared for by their married children. Their names are Louise and Hazel. Hazel's son, David, is married to Louise's daughter, Nancy. They both take care of their parents together in their home.

David takes care of his mother's needs. These needs include washing, ironing her clothes, cleaning her part of the house, taking her to her doctor appointments, and accompanying her while she shops for clothes. Hazel is ninety-one years old. She is a short heavy set woman with a dark skin complexion and silver grey hair worn in a short natural style. She is from New Orleans and speaks with the dialect of that region. She is a beautiful woman with no wrinkles on her body. She walks without a cane, although her son strongly insists that she does. She says,

"I may be ninety-one but I am still here."

And she proudly lets everybody know it.

Nancy takes care of her mother, Louise, with the aid of a care provider who comes in four days a week. The provider does light cleaning, washes, irons, helps Louise with her hygiene, picks out her clothes, and helps her to get dressed. She also takes her for walks as the weather permits. The care provider's last name is Love and she certainly lives up to that name. She respects Louise's independence by allowing her to do what she wants for herself and does so without scolding or reprimanding her for not asking for help. She lets Louise try to locate what she is looking for. When she can't find it Mrs. Love will retrieve it for her by placing the object Louise is trying to locate in her hand or in a place where the object can be easily found. Louise's bedroom is at the end of a small hallway with the bathroom to her left and her small living room to her right, which is adjacent to her bedroom. When Louise gets disoriented in trying to locate her bedroom, by going into the bathroom or living room accidently, her care provider is always near to direct her to the right room. When walking with Louise it is done with utmost respect; giving her dignity as a normal person instead of being treated like a handicap person.

Nancy takes care of her mother's medical needs by assuring her doctor's appointments and her prescriptions are current.

Louise is blind with hypertension and cannot hear well. She is from Arkansas and speaks with the dialect from that region. Her speech is slow and long, with the impression of taking forever to speak. She is very friendly with a perpetual smile. She is five feet tall with big eyes, thin lips, and weighs 108 pounds.

"I may be a small piece of leather, but I am well put together!" she tells people when teased about being so small.

In 2016, David and Nancy celebrated their forty-seventh wedding anniversary.

They decided to take their parents to Brookdale Assisted Living in Sugar Land, Texas, where they live.

They arrived before their appointment and were invited to lunch. Initially, Louise and Hazel were to get separate rooms but it was later decided for them to share a room since it was spacious enough to accommodate them both.

Nancy asked for permission to rearrange the room for the comfort of her mother due to her blindness. Her request was graciously granted. Nancy instructed for Louise's furniture be moved to the front of the room near the entrance door across from the bathroom. White typing paper was placed above the doorknob of the bathroom door. This made it easier for Louise to find the bathroom. Hazel's furniture remained in the back of the room, which gave them plenty of space to move about.

After changing the room for her mother's comfort, David and Nancy left to begin their vacation the next day.

Scene 1

Hazel is watching television and Louise is moving about in the room. She is feeling along the wall and tapping on furniture and doors.

Hazel: "Why are you feeling on them walls and hitting on them doors and furniture like you crazy?"

Louise: "I am orienting myself to the room."

Hazel: "You is doing what?"

Louise: "You know I am blind and this is the way I see."

Hazel: "I didn't know you was blind; nobody told me. Maybe if you take off them dark glasses you could see."

Louise: "That will not help! I have no light in my eyes. It is all dark."

Hazel often forgot that Louise was blind so Louise found her bed and sat down on it. A caregiver comes into the room with two call bells, in the form of necklaces, to put around Louise and Hazel's neck. She instructed them to push the button that hung from the center of the necklace should they need any assistance. She explained how it worked and informed them that this necklace must be worn throughout their entire stay there. She returned shortly.

Caregiver: "Yes, Mrs. Hazel. May I help you?"

Hazel: "Naw, I don't need any help. Why do you ask?"

Caregiver: "You pushed your call button."

Hazel: "I ain't pushed no button."

The care giver walks over and turns off the call button from the necklace around Hazel's neck.

Hazel: "What is this thing you got around my neck?"

The care giver explains again what the necklace was. Hazel was not impressed.

Hazel: "Here, take this thing. I don't need it!"

Caregiver: "Yes you do! Keep it around your neck."

She places the necklace around Hazel's neck again and leaves the room.

Hazel takes the necklace off of her neck and places it in her nightstand drawer.

Hazel: "I don't want this thing around my neck. No telling what it will do. She must thank I am crazy."

Scene 2

The caregiver comes to take Louise and Hazel to the dining room for dinner. She leads them to a table to wait for dinner to be served.

Louise hears a lot of noises in the room and asks Hazel,

Louise: "What is all this noise I am hearing? Describe this dining room to me..."

Hazel: "Alright. It is a very large room, something like a restaurant, with windows on both sides of the room and a lot of tables and chairs. This table has a number twelve on it so I guess this is the number of the table. The noises you are hearing are people talking and there's also a person rolling a cart with water, juice, tea, and coffee from table to table. There's also a server taking food orders.

The cart rolls to Louise and Hazel's table.

Server: "What would you like to drink, Mrs. Hazel?"

Hazel: "Juice, cranberry."

Next came the person taking orders.

Server: "What would you like for dinner? There are four choices that you may select from."

Hazel: "I will take the roasted chicken dinner."

Server: "And what would you like, Mrs. Louise?"

Louise: "I will take a vegetable plate with no meat and water."

The server continues taking orders from their table.

Louise: "How many people are sitting at our table?"

Hazel: "These tables are small with only seats for four. So there are two people sitting at our table with us."

Louise: "Are they black or white?"

Hazel: "White."

Louise thought she heard Hazel say 'black'.

"Good." Louise said to herself. "It will be easy to talk to them."

So she leaned over to the one to her left and said:

Louise: "Hi, my name is Louise. What is your name?"

Person: "My name is Dasey."

Louise addressed the person in front of her.

Louise: "And what is your name?"

Person: "Peggy."

Peggy began to sing a pretty little tune over and over.

Hazel: "And my name is Hazel. Pleased to meet y'all."

Louise: "Where are you from, Dasey?"

Dasey: "I am from Houston and where are you from?"

Louise: "I am from Oakland, California, but I was born in Arkansas. We left there in 1946. How long have you lived in Houston?"

Dasey: "I have lived here all of my life. I was born and raised in Houston."

Louise: "Wow, then you was here when the white folks wasn't too nice to the black folks. I don't know how you stayed here all of your life. We had to leave Arkansas. It was so bad for us black folks. You know how we had to get off of the sidewalk when a white person was approaching us."

Dasey does not respond and Louise continues.

16

Louise: "Did you learn how to speak Pig Latin? That was the language we spoke so the white folks wouldn't know what we were talking about." (Louise laughs.)

Dasey: "No, I didn't. My mother said that was not a language and was something made up by other people. My brother learned how to speak it and it would upset our mother when he spoke it around the house."

This did not sound right. No black mother would get upset about her child speaking Pig Latin. Well, not unless she was one of those stuck up mothers who thought of themselves above other blacks. But most others thought this was a fun language and would speak and teach it to their children. Louise said this is how she learned it.

So Louise leaned over and whispered to Hazel,

"Did you say the person sitting next to me is black?"

Hazel: "Naw, she white."

Louise lowered her head and began to eat. She was too embarrassed to continue to speak.

Scene 3

Louise and Hazel were told that breakfast was at eight o'clock in the morning. They had gotten up at six o'clock and got themselves ready. A knock came at the door. It was the care provider. Louise took hold to her arm and Hazel followed. The provider assisted them to table twelve, which would be their table throughout their respite.

Hazel: "You have a menu in front of you. Why don't you look at it to see what you would like to eat?"

Louise: "I can't. Why don't you do it for me?"

Hazel: "What's wrong? Can't you read?"

Louise: "Yes, I can read. I just can't see how to read."

Hazel: "What you mean you can't see how to read?"

Louise: "You know that I am blind."

Hazel: "I know no such thang. Nobody told me."

The server comes to the table.

Server: "What would you like for breakfast? We serve a two course meal; the first course is hot and cold cereal, toast, orange or cranberry juice and fruit. The second course: bacon or ham, sausage, hash brown potatoes or grits, eggs and toast, and pancakes."

Hazel: "I will have cold cereal, a banana, and orange juice."

Louise: "And I will have hot cereal, toast, orange juice and herbal tea."

Peggy and Dasey join them.

The server brings them their breakfast. Louise peels her banana and it is over ripe. She yells.

Hazel: "This banana is rotten!"

Server: "I will bring you another one."

Hazel has three bananas beside her bowl of cereal: the rotten one, the one Louise gave her, and the one the server brought her.

Peggy: "What are you going to do with all those bananas?"

Hazel: "I am going to eat them. What do you think?"

Peggy: "I think there are too many. You are already over weight."

Hazel: "Overweight! Who's overweight? Not me! I look good to myself and I don't care what nobody else thinks."

Peggy throws a piece of banana peeling into Hazel's cereal bowl.

Hazel: "What did you do that for?"

Hazel pushes her chair back, getting up on her wobbly legs to get in Peggy's face.

Hazel: "Listen here; you don't know who you is fooling with! I will knock the mess out of your behind!"

Two caregivers rush over to the table before Hazel swings on Peggy.

Caregiver: "What is wrong Mrs. Hazel? Calm down."

She places her arms around Hazel and sits her down in her chair.

Hazel: "I wasn't doing anything to her and she come throwing that banana peeling at me. The snagged tooth heifer... She don't know who she is fooling with! She will change that tune when I get through with her. I don't take no mess from nobody and I don't care who they are!"

Caregiver: "We understand and will see that this doesn't happen again."

Peggy left the room and breakfast continued as usual.

Scene 4

It is lunch time. Hazel, Louise and Dasey are sitting at the table that is set with a white table cloth. The table displayed a cloth napkin that was placed in a wine glass beside a dinner plate and silverware neatly arranged on the table. The table was accented with a lovely floral center piece. Hazel and Dasey were describing the table setting to Louise when in walked Peggy. It was a tense moment because nobody knew what would happen between Peggy and Hazel after the incident earlier that morning.

Hazel and Peggy greeted each other in a friendly voice as if nothing had happened.

Hazel: "Good afternoon and how are you?"

Peggy: "I am fine and how are you?"

Hazel: "Fine as wine! You know I am fine because wine is good for you. Do you like wine?"

Peggy sat down and they began a conversation about wine; likewise with Louise and Dasey. They continued to talk as if Louise had not thought Dasey was black. They remained table companions throughout Hazel and Louise's respite at the facility.

After three days Hazel had become familiar with her surroundings. She knew how to walk the long hallway to her room, which is the last room at the end of the hall. She can go to the dining room without assistance and to the entertainment room where bingo and other entertainment is held.

Entertainment such as socializing with one another over happy hour treats, ice cream, cold drinks and snacks each Friday evening. Most of the residents looked forward to partaking in these occasions. Hazel attended all social functions, including exercise, church on Sunday and bible study once a week.

Louise wasn't as sociable as Hazel. She enjoyed listening to her talking books and radio.

One afternoon, just before dinner, Louise was in her room, relaxing listening to her radio. Suddenly the door opened and in walked Hazel with their granddaughter Katherine and her husband Jones.

Katherine: "Hi Nana! Sha-sha brought us to y'alls room with no problem. She knew where she was going."

Louise was lying across the bed listening to her radio. She had taken off her curly brown wig. She jumped up and said:

Louise: "Wait a minute. Let me put on my wig."

Louise pats around on the night stand where she had placed her wig.

Jones: "That's alright Nana. You don't have to put on your wig."

Katherine: "Let her put it on. She will feel better."

"Look better" is what Louise knew her granddaughter meant.

Louise found her wig and put it on her head, then sat down to visit with their granddaughter and her husband.

Katherine: "Sha-sha appears to like it here. She was the center of attention when we found her in a room laughing and talking with her peers."

She turned around to see what everybody was looking at and shouted,

"Katherine what are you doing here?"

Then she introduces us to the people in the room.

Sha-sha is the name Hazel's grandchildren call her. It means 'grandmother'.

Louise: "Yes, we like it here. The staff and residence are very nice. However, I did tell them about Hazel and Peggy's altercations. She had forgotten it and said I was lying on her. She would never do anything like that. I guess there are some benefits to dementia-forgetfulness."

At four o'clock a knock on the door reminded us that it was time for dinner. We were accompanied by our grandchildren to the dining room with Hazel leading the way.

Scene 5

Before breakfast Louise and Hazel were assisted to the medicine room to take their medicine. After they took their medicine Louise waited for the nurse's aide to come and assist her to the dining room. Someone took a hold of three of her fingers. She smelled Hazel's perfume.

Louise: "Hazel, is this you?"

Hazel: "Yea, come with me to the dining room. I will take you."

Hazel held on to Louise's hand and began walking out of the small medicine room. Louise called to the medical nurse.

Louise: "She can't take me to the dining room."

Medical nurse: "Yes she can. She knows where it is."

Louise is apprehensive and hesitates.

Hazel: "Come on! You thank I don't know where the dining room is?"

She began to walk, still holding Louise's fingers.

Louise: "Wait... Hazel, let me hold your arm. I can follow you better."

Hazel: "That's alright. I got you."

Louise goes along with Hazel. When entering the dining room entrance Louise bumps into a chair and table.

Hazel: "What is the matter with you? Didn't you see that chair and table? Come on."

Hazel never let go of Louise's fingers. She led her to the opposite side of the room.

Hazel: "Here is our table and chair. Sit down."

Hazel went to the front of the small table and sat down. This left Louise standing by the side of the table trying to locate the chair.

Louise: "Where is the chair, Hazel?"

Medical Nurse: "Here it is."

She pulls the chair from the table and helps Louise to sit in it.

The medical nurse had followed Louise and Hazel to the dining room after noticing Louise's apprehensiveness of Hazel assisting her to the dining room.

Hazel and Louise enjoyed their respite period at the Brookdale Assisted Living Facility. Louise said she would recommend this respite period to all caregivers of their loved ones, especially their aging parents. It is a frightening thing witnessing the aging or the entering into a second childhood, as claimed by some, for older people. But, this is not true. There is no second childhood. The parent is just not capable of doing the things they were once capable of doing when they were younger. However, if a parent is treated like a child, he or she may revert to a childlike manner or the parent will rebel and cause trouble for the caretaker. Some parents will refuse to be treated like a child. For instance, to treat Hazel like a child would be worse than her dementia.

Hazel and Louise are thankful for how their daughter-in-law and son-in-law take care of them. They allow them to do what they are capable of doing for themselves and assist them with what they can't do. They also encourage them to get out of the house and go to the senior citizen center on the senior bus that picks them up. Louise is 88 years old and Hazel is 91 years old. Louise's care provider accompanies them to the center. Arts and crafts are taught, along with other activities. Hazel is very sociable and enjoys socializing with her peers. Louise is limited to most activities because of her blindness, but she enjoys sitting among the art class and the teaching that occurs during the Bible class. Hazel is making Christmas gifts in the art class to give to the family for Christmas. The aging are no longer sitting in a rocking chair nor are they too weak and frail to help themselves. Many are up and about doing things even at the age of ninety-seven. There will be more discussion about this in the following chapters, which will be narrated by the author.

Part
2

Chapter 1: A New World of Aging and Care

We are indeed living in a new world of aging and care giving. The life expectancy age a century ago was three score and ten years. Living beyond this age was thought to be living on borrowed time. For the past decades this belief has been proven wrong. The life expectancy years has increased far beyond this predicted age. Hazel and I have certainly lived far beyond seventy years and many are living to the age of 100. There is a woman going into a senior citizen center who is106 years old.

I have never met this woman, but I am acquainted with another lady who attended the same church as I did. She lived to be 107 years old. The woman said that she was very sick with cancer in her early years. The doctor told her that she could not live much longer with that disease. She told the doctor that she would live to reach 100 and that she was not going to die. The doctor told her that the day she reached 100 years of living he would take her to dinner. The day she reached 100 years of age she called the doctor, who was an old man himself by then, and told him that he could take her dinner because she was now 100 years old. Not only did she go to dinner with the doctor, but seven years later she went to the voting poll to vote for Barack Obama to become the President of the United States. Pictures were taken of her going into the voting booth.

I decided to look into this phenomenal growth of aging people, which is far beyond the aging of people a century ago. For instance, in the 1800's life expectancy after birth was age 32. It grew to age 41 in 1850, 50 in 1900, and 57 years of age in 1950. What happened to bring about this difference in aging? It is no secret; a better lifestyle. Healthy living, better sanitation, and healthier diets are all assets that help one live better. There has been a one hundred percent improvement in sanitation. Where there wasn't access to running water in houses, many people didn't take baths. In fact, some had never taken a bath in their lives. The Saturday night baths were no joke. I was around when baths were taken only on Saturday nights in tin washtubs. All the children in the family took a bath first using the same bath water and then adding warm water to the previous bath water. This was done until all had rotated and taken a bath in the same water. The last person to take a bath had the most water to bathe with. Homemade soap made with lye was used. Later, it was recommended that bathes should be taken twice a week. This is not to say that no one cleansed themselves just because they only took a bath once a week. For those who were well off they had a pitcher with water and a basin, in which they could wash their face, hands, and other body parts. The poorer classes used a dipper to pour water from a bucket into a washing pan to clean them. Once the sanitation problem was solved and running water was pumped or piped into some houses, health sanitation continued to improve even until today. This could be the cause of the growth of seniors over 85 years of age globally.

The changing of the diet also appeared to improve the lives of aging individuals. A proper diet of vegetables and less meat was advocated, as well as increased water consumption, exercise, and proper rest. Abstinence from drinking alcohol, and chewing and smoking tobacco was also encouraged. These reforms greatly helped to reduce 'health problems', as they were called in the good old days; decades ago. Following through on those health practices appears to have manifested good health to many older people today. It has encouraged them to be more active, work longer, and help themselves with little or no assistance from their children or others. There are some old seniors who refuse to retire or discontinue work because of their age.

An 82 year old man asked the church and prayer line to pray for him to get a job because his fixed income was not enough to cover his expenses. Many prayed and some doubted that a man his age would be hired on a job but he was. In fact, he was offered two jobs. One was driving a taxi cab, since his former job was as a truck driver. Later he was offered a job at Walmart, not as a greeter as one would expect, but as a warehouseman working in the warehouse. He was a man who followed the eight laws of health; getting plenty of fresh air, sunshine, exercise, eight glasses of water a day, six to eight hours of rest, a proper diet of fruits, vegetables, grains and nuts, temperance, good thought, and prayer. He neither looked nor acted like an eighty-two year old man. He was friendly, outgoing, and a man of faith who loved the Lord.

Another young, old single senior woman, who refused to retire, applied for a government job. She passed the test and was hired at the age of 70. She said that although she was the oldest person on the job it didn't bother her because she was capable of keeping up with the rest of them. She also doesn't look her age because she follows the eight laws of health. She is neither sickly nor weak, and appears to have as much energy as her coworkers. She said she plans to remain at this job until she is 80 years old and then she will think of retirement.

This is possible. My daughter, a teacher, worked with an older teacher who retired at the age of 83. She was never absent due to illness and was always on time. She had a sharp mind all the way up to the time she retired and beyond.

Another courageous widow lost her husband after 60 years of marriage. They had no children, so she was left alone with only her husband's relatives. Many of them were of the third generation and didn't know her too well. So she decided to move back to her hometown in Houston to be with her relatives, only to find the same dilemma; third generation children who knew nothing about her. Most of her relatives and peers had passed away. Only one cousin was left there. So she moved backed to the small town in California where she had spent her 60 years of marriage. She said that she was alone in her previous hometown, which had become a strange place to her after so many years away. If she was going to be alone it might as well be in a town that she was familiar with. She was 83 years old when her husband passed away and was about 85 years old when she moved back to California. She had sold her home and needed a place to stay. She didn't want to stay in an assistance living facility so she stayed at the Holiday Inn until she found a house. Once the house was found, she moved in and lived there alone. She was capable of caring for her by washing, cleaning her house, cooking, and riding the city bus to shop and take care of her personal affairs.

She went to church and met a woman there who became a dear friend to her. Now she no longer has to catch the city bus for shopping or tend to her affairs. Her friend takes her where she needs to go and calls her every morning and night to see if all is well with her. She praises God, for now she is not alone. This widow is now 95 years old and appears to be content. She always answers her phone with a friendly laughter. She is still very active as she cooks for herself and cleans her house. One day she climbed up a ladder to hang curtains in the window and fell. She didn't tell anyone because she realized that she shouldn't have been on that ladder. God was with her because she didn't break her hip. She laughed and said,

"God takes care of old folks and fools."

Another widow is 92 years old and is a mother of six children. Two of the children are demised and four are living far away from her. A daughter lives in California and a son and daughter lives in Georgia. Although she lives in California with her son and daughter, they live in a different city. This however doesn't stop her from seeing them. She flies often to Georgia to see her son and daughter. They drive her to see her siblings in Louisiana. She spends time with them and then flies back to California. Her daughter in California visits her often and wants her mother to come and live with her but the mother prefers to live in her own home. This widow likes to fish, so she gets in a boat and would go fishing with her son every day if she could. She drove her car until her children thought she was too old to drive. So she sold her car to please them. Not satisfied with being chauffeured around town by other people she decided to buy herself another car. She drove herself around town while promising her children that she would not drive on the freeway.

These are just a few old-old seniors in today's world that I know who have taken their lives into their own hands and are doing things that their family and others didn't think they were capable of doing.

I received a phone call from a church member whom I had not heard from for many years.

"I ran across your name and phone number while sorting through some papers and thought I would call to see if you still had this phone number. I have just moved into a larger house. I couldn't stay in that small house my children moved me in to for the past two years. This is a much bigger house. It's a three bedroom house with a family room, living room, dining room, two baths, and a very large kitchen. This is more of what I am use to. I have a large master bedroom with a walk in closet, a guest bedroom and I will take the third bedroom for my office. I also have a large back and front yard and a two car garage. I can still drive my car around town and to attend church. Just because I am 84 years old doesn't mean I don't like nice things. I plan to remain here for the next ten years. Then my children can do what they want with me. I will be 94 by then so it won't matter, I guess."

I couldn't imagine an 84 year old woman moving in to a house that large all alone, even though she is one who observes the eight laws of health and is most likely in the best of health.

It is not too surprising to see women living by themselves as old seniors, but not many men appear to be able to live alone without someone caring for them. However, there is one gentleman that I must write about. It was my grandfather. He was quite the character, and lived to the age of 102. At 65 years old he and his wife moved from Detroit to Southern California, bought a home and he became a gardener. He specialized in cutting lawns until age 75. Grandmother said he was always busy and when she called for him to come in and eat he could not be found. Later she would see him coming down the street with a wheelbarrow full of bull...mess, which he used for fertilizer. He was very healthy because he ate from his garden from which he had planted many vegetables such as corn, collard greens, turnip greens, okra, beets, green beans, squash, onions, etc.

After grandmother died he lived alone, caring for himself until the age of 95. The neighborhood began to complain about this old man living by himself. They were afraid that something would happen to him because he still continued his daily tasks with no signs of fatigue. He consistently took care of his garden, went shopping, riding the city bus, and going to the bank while carrying large sums of money with him. His son carried him home to live with him. When he reached 100 years old I asked him how it felt to be 100.

"I don't know," he said.

"I have never been 100 years old before."

He lived to be 102 years old. His son put him in a dependent living facility when he was 99 years old because he kept running away from the house. He posed as a problem because he kept flirting with the nurses. But he remained there until death.

Another older gentleman I know was quite charming in his younger days. He was tall and I do mean tall, dark, and very handsome. He was about six feet and five inches and always dressed in a blue or black suit that fitted his tall medium frame very well. He had, and still does have a charming smile, that showed his gold crown front tooth. He was very talkative and friendly. I

48

don't think he ever met a stranger. He was friendly to everyone he met with his loud voice. I think he lived alone until in his mid-90's when his sister, who was then living, worried about him because he never conducted himself like an old man. He was still driving in his red Honda civic, flying back and forth from Texas, Arkansas, and Oklahoma. He was loyal in visiting his siblings each year from the time he was a young man. She had forbidden him from traveling alone at his age; to this he took no heed, but kept flying. However this year, 2016, at the age of 96, he will not be flying alone. Instead, his niece, his sister's daughter, will be flying with him. They first landed in Dallas, Texas and his niece rented a car to drive him to visit his other siblings in Arkansas, Oklahoma and also to Sugar Land, Texas. There he visited David, Nancy and their parents. Then they flew back to California. His niece said she thought this trip would be exhausting to him, but it wasn't. He tolerated it very well. She said she doesn't know when he will think he is too old to travel because shortly after arriving home he wanted to go on a trip to Reno with his church family for an outing. After nine o'clock that night his niece, who also accompanied him there, was ready to retire for the night. Not her uncle! He didn't retire until 2 a.m. the next morning.

In November 2016, this older gentleman will be 97 years old and shows no signs of slowing down, so I am told. His only problem, he laughingly says, is that his ears are not working too well. He also is diabetic, but he doesn't let that stop him from doing what he wants to do. He likes to eat out, so he gets in his little red Honda Civic car and drives himself to his favorite restaurant to eat.

Chapter 2: Senior Care

Although there are many old seniors who are capable of caring for themselves and tending to their affairs fairly well, there are many seniors who need constant care twenty-four seven. Fortunately, there is no need for them to feel sorrowful or afraid, due to the fact that an enterprise has been created for the sole purpose of supporting those who cannot care for themselves. We are living in a new world of care. Just a few decades ago, there were only two options of care for the aging.

1. They could either be cared for by their family at home.
2. If the finance, stress or strain became too heavy they could be sent to a nursing home. This is something no family wanted to do, but sometimes it was the only option.

Today there are so many options to choose from, including government help.

Some may need assistance in choosing which option is best for their aging parents and others. Since I am among the aging parents, under the care of my only daughter, I have continued my research to see what was best and available for Hazel and me. Diligently searching I discovered industries of care for the aging. So as not to get confused I looked into the classification of aging people to see what stage Hazel and I were in for the help we needed in our declining years. For instance, people between the ages of 65 and 74 are considered the young-old. People between the ages of 75 and 84 are considered the middle-old, and the old-old are above the age of 85.

Although predictions can be made about the change according to the individual aging rate as determined, as children grow at certain rates, so do aging seniors. Although Hazel and I are in the category of the old-old, me being 88 and Hazel being 91, we can still manage self care. Self care meaning being able to independently bathe and dress ourselves, and use the toilet with little or no help. However, we are not able to maintain daily living on our own such as home care, shopping, and taking care of our affairs. We are thankful that we are changing at a slow rate, which will give our children time to select the best care for whatever changes may occur in our lives. Although Hazel and I have lost a certain amount of our sensorial awareness's, we are very thankful that we have not yet leaned to the end of the spectrum of old where we cannot do anything for ourselves. Thank God, we are aging gracefully.

Chapter 3: Aging Gracefully

An elderly man once said,

"I am just waiting to die."

Aging, however, is not a death sentence, nor is it a punishment. It is just the body slowing down to age gracefully if given the proper care. Hazel and I are aging gracefully with the proper care from our children.

I have been living with my daughter Nancy and son-in-law David, for twelve years now. Nancy and David moved to Sugar Land, Texas in 2004. At the age of 76 I followed shortly after. Living with my daughter and son-in-law was the best time of my life. Nancy and I shopped every day and she took me to church every Sabbath where I gained a lot of friends. I was not sickly; my only health problems were hypertension and glaucoma, which lead to my blindness at the age of 85. Hazel has only been living with us for the past three years. In the past, David would visit her once or twice a year. He began to notice that her behavior was changing each time he visited and wanted her to come to Texas to live with him and his family. Even though Hazel didn't want to live in Texas, her living alone wasn't going so well. She attended her granddaughter's wedding in 2013 but her illness worsened and she had to be hospitalized. She has been with the family ever since.

When David and Nancy realized that their parents would be living with them, they immediately began to safeguard their two story house. They installed a chair lift on the seventeen stairs that we would have had to walk up and down. They also safeguarded the bathrooms by mounting guardrails along the bathtub wall, setting rubber mats in each of our bathtubs, and placing non-skid rugs on the floor. When I became blind they also made a pathway for me throughout the house. At this time, I was 85 and Hazel was 88. Our children treated us like two queens. They cooked breakfast and dinner every day while sitting back to watch us enjoy our meal, which they prepared with love. We called them "Chef Nancy" and "Chef David" because they cooked the very best food for us. When they did not feel like cooking they took us to the best restaurants in town. Yet, with all of this proper care, Hazel and I are still declining in age. Keeping in mind that our children are in the young-old stage of their lives, I decided to continue to research the best place for Hazel and me to go to help relieve our children from more stress and strain than was necessary.

Chapter 4: Senior Centers and Senior Day Care Centers

I asked my daughter to look for a Senior Center for Hazel and me to go during the day. She did and located a very nice center where Hazel and I could go and exercise, socialize with our peers, receive nutritious meals, and play bingo; which Hazel loves to do. There were many other interesting and updated projects that we could participate in as well.

We were fortunate that my daughter selected the right center for us. Later I learned that there are two different types of senior centers:

1. Senior Citizen Centers
2. Senior Adult Day Care Centers.

It would have been a discouraging experience for us to wind up in the wrong center. Senior Citizen Centers are for those with good physical and mental health; some as young as 55 years of age. Senior Adult Day Care Centers are for those with aging physical disabilities, frailties, and early stages of dementia. They may be getting help at home, but can come to the center during the day were they receive valuable physical and mental stimulation. It is good to know the difference between the two centers. Although Hazel and I are not in excellent health, with her in early stages of dementia and I being blind, we still have fairly good physical health left in us. Hazel is very friendly and can go about the center on her own. I, on the other hand, need my care provider to lead me around the center. I still have a fair amount of mental coordination and I love to socialize with my peers.

I know if Hazel and I keep aging than our next place will be the Senior Adult Day Care Center, which I am willing to go to in order to relieve our children of the unnecessary strain and stress of caring for us, especially with them approaching the middle-old stage of their lives.

Let me explain more about the senior adult day care center. It is a place to care for those who are physically frail and in early dementia. Should Hazel's dementia progress from memory loss, to confusion, to a childlike stage and my blindness progress to the stage where I may need more assistance with eating, finding things, and dressing myself, than an Adult Center would give great assistance to us while we remain in our children's home. We can be transported to the Adult Day Care Center to give respite for Nancy and David. The center offers physical stimulation and some medical care. The adult must be ambulatory and must not be incontinent or physically impaired. Although the center is a non-profit organization, the cost is arranged from $25 to $100 dollars a day, depending upon in condition of the person.

Although it is good to know about the availability of these centers, I would like to go into an assistant living facility because it is the next best care from home. It is not the same as a hospital or nursing care home where nurses follow a regiment of rules and regulations concerning your care. In an assistant living facility, care is needed, but the resident still has his or her independence. They are not told when to go to bed, when to dress or when to get up. Should they not want to eat in the dining room, then food is brought directly to their room. There are no nurses hovering over them, but staff is always on standby to see that no harm comes to residents, and they are ready to assistant when needed.

I know of a widow who has seven adult children. They are all professional college graduates. She lived alone in her own home and developed an early stage of dementia. Her eldest daughter noticed a change in her behavior and seeing that her mother could no longer remain alone in her home she called a meeting with her siblings. They all were living in different states, while working and raising their own families. They decided to place their mother in an Independent Living Center apartment where she could take her own furniture, such as her large screen TV, piano and bedroom furniture. She remained in this facility until her dementia progressed to where she needed more help in her everyday living and she was moved to assistant living. Then, when her second oldest daughter's two sons were in college she brought her mother home to live with her family. This was the best decision the siblings could make for the care of their aging mother at the time. However, if bringing her mother home to live with her family doesn't work, there are other options that can be made. A few years ago those options were not as available as they are today. This is good, as it gives the one who is now the care giver of their loved one the assurance that she or he is not alone.

The fastest growing population in American is that of the old-old, people who are 85 years old and up. This group of aging seniors is projected to grow from 4.6 million people in 2002 to 9.6 million in 2030 and double that in the year 2050. However, the enterprise for caring for the aging has also grown prodigiously. Nursing care homes, nonmedical caregivers to do light cleaning, cooking and caring for your loved one and medical nurses who care for the medical needs of your loved one are just a few examples of the options that one has for the care of the aging. When the aging parent can no longer remain at home, there are many other provisions that can be arranged for him or her.

It is best to have purchased a long term health insurance plan in your early age, but, of course if most people were like me, they would not have thought to buy this type of insurance while they were young, due to assuming that they would never reach an old age anyway. People in my day only had two options. They could either take care of their aged, or send them to the nursing home, which was considered a waiting place next to the grave because the nursing home in those days were in very poor conditions and overrun with patients and an understaffing of nurses.

There was an older woman in her 90's with both legs amputated below the knees. She lived alone, with only her son to take care of her. He was married and lived in a small town not far from her home, but he could not attend to her every day. She didn't want to go into a nursing home and made him promise that he would not send her to one. He and a few church members attended to her needs whenever they could. She left the front door unlocked day and night so that those who came to help her could come in because she couldn't let them in. She couldn't do anything for herself but sit in her bed waiting for help. There weren't many young people in the church to help her because the younger generation didn't know her and most of her peers were deceased.

Her grandson, who lived in another state, came to see her and saw the sad condition she was in. He immediately took her to a nursing home. His grandmother screamed at and rebuked her son for letting her grandson take her from her home. However, she soon discovered that the nursing home was far better the treatment she was receiving at home. In her day and time, a nursing home was a place where one went to die it seemed and this is why she didn't want to go to a nursing home. But time has truly changed.

I would personally prefer going into an independent living facility, as this is one of the next best options to living at home. You are mostly on your own. You can go to bed or get up whenever you wish. The aid is only there to assist you and a medical nurse gives medication as needed. You also get three meals a day and entertainment all throughout the day. However, this facility is expensive. This is where long term insurance comes in if you have it because most living facilities don't take Medicare, nor does Medicare even pay for this type of care. The next best place is the nursing care home, which has fewer patients, but can also be expensive. As one continues to decline in age, where he or she is no longer able to care for him or herself, a skilled nursing home is where he or she can be placed. Money or health insurance plans should have been made to receive such care as this, but, if not other alternatives can be arranged.

Chapter 5: Medicare and Medicaid Government Insurance Plans

As I mentioned before, I neglected to purchase a health insurance plan in my early age. I didn't expect to live past the age of 55 and living to the age of 65 was simply out of the question for me. Now I am at the age of 88; an age that no one in my mother's family lived to. So here I am in the care of my daughter and her husband without health insurance. I only have Medicare and Medicaid, which are federal and state insurances, respectively. This insurance is available to all adults beginning at the age of 65. When I reached 65 I immediately applied for Medicare because I thought this was what I was to do. I wasn't sick or frail and I was always filled with energy and health. I was also very active. I never gave age a thought. One day, I was in a hurry to get to the store before it closed. I tried to run fast, but my legs wouldn't move as quickly as I expected. That's when I remembered I was 75 years old.

At the age of 65 I also applied for social security, which in my case wasn't much because I tried to work on jobs that gave the weekends off. In this way, I could stay true to my belief in keeping the seventh-day Sabbath Holy. Consequently, I mostly worked at low paying jobs where I could get the Sabbath off.

With such low income from social security I was eligible for the state health insurance plan named Medi-Cal. It was a state health plan in California. When I moved to the state of Texas I was entitled to the same plan, only it was named Medicaid.

Medicare and Medicaid are primarily for those with little or no income. To be eligible for Medicaid, the state health insurance, one must not have assets over $2,000.00. This includes any amount of money over $2,000.00, including money in the bank or in your pocket.

In my research about Medicaid I discovered that Medicaid is a mean tested welfare program designed for the poor of all ages, including the aging. For those under 65 years old, Medicaid generally pays the cost for medical bills such as maternity for poor women and pediatric care for their children. For those over 65, it will help pay the nursing home cost once they have exhausted all or almost all their means. Medicaid will only pay for certified nursing home care.

For a private room in some nursing homes it costs $212.00 a day, which adds up to$77,380 a year. Semi-private rooms cost $191 a day; $69,715.00 a year. $4,000.00 to $6,000.00 a month is what one must pay to live in an assistant living facility, as of this writing. For 20 days, Medicare will pay full payment for a hospital stay and eighty percent thereafter for 100 days. Medicaid will pay for the twenty percent that Medicare doesn't pay. I am told that most assistant living facilities don't except Medicare and Medicaid. When I was accepted into the state insurance plan, Medicaid, I read the policy thoroughly to get information as to how it worked. I was surprised at all the help it afforded. Medical transportation, rehabilitation care, home nursing care, and partial pharmaceutical payments are just a few of the services that were offered. Read your Medicare policy and book, which are sent yearly with all the information it gives to help. Some people do not receive the full benefits allotted to them because they do not read what is available for them.

Although one may not be able to receive top of the line health care due to the lack of funds, help is available. However, you must know how to access it. There are also programs to help those who have special needs and can't afford to pay for the need.

Before I lost my sight completely I was introduced to a program for the blind name DARS (Department of Rehabilitation Services). It is a program that trains you on how to survive without sight. This training proved to be successful after I lost my sight. Read my next book on Journey into Darkness.

Chapter 6: Hospice Care

This is one sure thing that will happen to every living person; death. No one likes to talk about it, but as sure as one has life, he or she will face death sooner or later. So why not discuss it while you can? With aging on the rise, no one knows how long he or she will live. As my Grandfather said when he reached the age of one hundred,

"I didn't know I would live this long."

Hazel and I have already lived to get into the old-old age group and how much longer we will live; we don't know. So while I am in my right mind I want to talk about the end. My daughter and son- in-law have seen to it that I am living a good life so they might as well take it to the end. I want to relieve them of unnecessary grief and pain because they are doing their best to make me comfortable during my declining years.

I want it to be known, then and now, that I do not want to be connected to any life support machine with tubes connected to prolonging my life when I am already gone. Years ago death was determined by the stopping of the heart and the inability to resuscitate it. Today I am told that death is determined by the brain. As long as there is life in the brain, there is no death. The brain must be completely dead. A patient can remain on a life support for years. I do not want this to happen to me.

I called a dear friend one evening and heard singing, talking and laughter in the background.

"Where are you," I asked. At a party?

"No," she replied. "My sister is in the hospital and we are here to comfort her until the end."

If this happens to me I want to leave exactly like that; with dignity and grace.

Hazel and I have lived a long life with no regret. Most of our friends and loved ones have passed away. On February 22, 2017 I turned 89 years old and Hazel turned 92 on April 2, 2017.

"And we're still here!" Hazel said. "So we must have one something right."

Epilogue

Although Hazel and I have lived a happy and fulfilled life, her dementia has progressed to where she is now living at the Brookdale Living Facility. This is the place where we spent our respite period when David and Nancy went on their vacation. David was pleased with the care his mother received at this Independent Living Facility. So much so that he returned her back to live there. This was a good choice because Hazel appears to adjust well and is happy among her peers.

Although her dementia continues to progress to where her memory is greatly impaired it appears to be manageable by the staff.

Louise is still home with her daughter and son in-in-law but she doesn't know when she will be next to leaving, as she continues to decline in age.

"But I am not worried," she said.

I have three more books to write; *Journey Into Darkness*, the sequel to *Oneda*, and *Going Home* (journey back to Arkansas). I hope to complete these books before I reach age 100. That will be eleven years from now, which is plenty of time to complete the three books. Many older seniors today are not afraid to follow their dream regardless of their age. After all, these are the baby boomers that are beginning to age alone with the Great Depression generation.

J.P. Jones, a retired carpenter of many years, decided to return back to college at the age of 70 to fulfill his dream of becoming a lawyer. He registered into college and was accepted. He completed two semesters and became sick and had to discontinue. He said he would return when his health improved.

We are living in a new world of ageing example. Ageing is not a death sentence; it is just a part of life God has given you. I am 89 at the time of this writing. I have many plans to fulfill and I have no time to worry about ageing. Ageing is just the number of days you are spending upon this earth, so don't worry about the years. Many people are paralyzed with fear of getting old but they shouldn't. Ageing is just the beginning of a new life style. Getting an education, marrying, raising children, and grandchildren is old. It is now time to begin a new life style. Be you; married or single.

I was 79 years old when I wrote my first book and 82 years old when I became an author. I became visually impaired at age 85 but this did not discourage me. I am still an author with many other books to write.

Appendix 1

NEWSTART: GOD'S LAWS OF HEALTH

Are you looking for a fresh NEW START in your health? God's 8 Laws of Health - which is the NEW START program of: Nutrition * Exercise * Water * Sunshine * Temperance* Rest * Air * and Trust in God. * These are God's Natural Remedies! Much of what is written on God's 8 Laws of Health - the NEW START program - Nutrition, Exercise, Water, Sunshine, Temperance, Rest, Air and Trust in God was written by Ellen White. She wrote extensively on God's Natural Remedies. Most of the quotes have a date by them... check it out...you will be amazed at the light she had so early in time! As early as 1868 she

was telling people that meat eating was the cause of cancer and was not safe to eat! And it 1899, she said it wouldn't be long and milk and dairy products would no longer be safe! Science and Doctors are just catching up to her with all the scientific information supporting exactly what she said in regards to the safety of meat eating and dairy products and the rest of God's Natural Remedies.

I. NUTRITION

Dangers of Meat Eating and Dairy Products

"The following list of common complaints can be directly linked to the consumption of meat and dairy products : hives, sinusitis, heart disorders, seborrhea, impaired digestion, obesity, dermatitis, diarrhea, edema, acne, gas and bloating, body odor, dry scaly skin, constipation, allergies, bedwetting, fatigue, hyperactivity, colitis attacks, headaches, colic, depression, anger, congestion and runny nose, irritability, excess mucus, hemorrhoids, impotence, ma-labsorption, hormone imbalance and hot flashes!" Prescription for Dietary Wellness, pgs. 144-147.

"The liability to take disease is increased tenfold by meat-eating." Counsels on Diet and Foods, pg. 386. (1868).

"The intellectual, the moral, and the physical powers are depreciated by the habitual use of flesh meats. Meat-eating deranges the system beclouds the intellect, and blunts the moral sensibilities. We say to you, dear brother and sister, your safest course is to let meat alone." Counsels on Diet and Foods, pg. 391 (1868).

"The tissues of the swine swarm with parasites. Of the swine, God said, "It is unclean unto you; ye shall not eat of their flesh, or touch their dead carcass." This command was given because swine's flesh is unfit for food. Swine are scavengers, and this is the only use they were intended to serve. Never, under any circumstances, was their flesh to be eaten by human beings."

Counsels on Diet an Foods, pg. 392. (1905)

"7 out o 10 people who eat pork have trichina antibodies in their blood streams." Dr. Agatha Thrash, Uchee Pines Institute.

BLV - Bovine Leukemia Virus - is on the rise in the US. 20% of adult dairy cows have it and 60% of dairy and beef herds surveyed are infected with BLV. More than 47% - almost half- of the dairy cows in Florida were found to be infected with BLV. That is the highest concentration in the world other than Venezuela!

Grains

It is much healthier to use whole grains, not refined ones. No white flour, white pasta, white rice, white bread , etc. "THE WHITER THE BREAD ....THE SOONER YOU'RE DEAD!!!"

Whole grains are good for all blood sugar disorders. Make sure that the bread label says the word "whole" and not just "wheat", otherwise it is really just plain old white flour.

It's very important to vary your grains...don't eat the same grain every day. Most people have wheat every day. Try adding Spelt, Kamut, Corn, Barley, Millet, Rice, Rye or even more exotic grains Amaranth or Quinoa.

Grains should be thoroughly cooked or baked. Raw grains are not healthy. Many people are allergic to gluten - the protein in the wheat and other grains. Grains that do not contain gluten are: Rice, Corn, Quinoa and Amaranth.

Sugar

Sugar is not good for the stomach. It causes fermentation, and this clouds the brain and brings peevishness into the disposition." Counsels on Diet and Foods , pg. 327. (1901)

"Free sugar has been shown to reduce the ability of white blood cells to function properly, to aggravate heart disease, to reduce lifespan, to contribute to alcoholism, mental illness, high blood pressure, skin disease, and enlarged liver and kidneys." Nutrition for Vegetarians., pg. 39. (Dr. Agatha Thrash).

Sugar is "food for cancer."

Believe it or not - back in the 1800's sugar was "by prescription ONLY".

Healthy Sugars: Barley Malt, Brown Rice Syrup, Honey, Date Sugar, Molasses, Fructose, Stevia

II. EXERCISE

"In order for the brain to have clearness and strength of thought retentive memory, and mental power, the muscles of the body should have exercise a portion of each day in order to preserve and improve health." The Health Reformer, March 1, 1873. (Ellen White)

"When the weather will permit, all who can possibly do so ought to walk in the open air every day, summer and winter. But the clothing should be suitable for the exercise, and the feet should be well protected. A walk, even in winter, would be more beneficial to the health than all the medicine the doctors may prescribe. For those who can walk, walking is preferable to riding. The muscles and veins are enabled better to perform their work. There will be increased vitality, which is so necessary to health. The lungs will have needful action; for it is impossible to go out in the bracing air of a winter's morning without inflating the lungs." Counsels on Health, pg. 552.

"The chief if not the only reason why many become invalids is that the blood does not circulate freely, and the changes in the vital fluid, which are necessary to life and health, do not take place. They have not given their bodies exercise not their lungs food, which is pure, fresh air, therefore it is impossible for the blood to be vitalized., and it pursues its course sluggish through the system. The more we exercise, the better will be the circulation of the blood. More people die for want of exercise than through over - fatigue; very man more rust out than wear out. Those who accustom themselves to proper exercise in the open air, will generally have a good and vigorous circulation. We are more dependent upon the air we breathe than upon the food we eat. Men and women, young and old, who desire health and who would enjoy active life, should remember that they cannot have these without a good circulation. Whatever their business and inclinations are, they should make up their minds to exercise in the open air as much as they can." (Ellen White).

III. WATER

Drink at least 8 glasses of water a day.

"Pure water to drink and fresh air to breathe invigorate the vital organs, purifies the blood, and helps nature in her task of overcoming the bad conditions of the system." (Ellen White).

Many health problems would be eliminated, including bowel and bladder problems, anxiety attacks, and food tolerance reactions, burning in the stomach, headaches, colitis pain, hot flashes and many other problems IF enough water were drunk.

Water flushes out the toxins that cause many health problems.

If those who are afflicted would assist nature in her effort by the use of pure, soft water , much suffering would be prevented." (Ellen White).

Drinking lots of pure water everyday will

definitely help to prevent cancer.

IV. SUNSHINE

This (sunshine) is one of nature's most healing agents." (Ellen White)

"If all would appreciate the sunshine, and expose every article of clothing to its drying, purifying rays, mildew and mold would be prevented....This is the only way rooms can be kept from impurities....Every room in our dwellings should be daily thrown open to the healthful rays of the sun and the purifying air should be invited in. This will be a preventive of disease." Health Reformer Articles. (Ellen White)

Many have become afraid of the sun, thinking they will get skin cancer from it. We believe that the sun does not cause skin cancer (unless you are constantly out in it, burning yourself), but rather, it is a purifier.....it brings to the surface (which is your skin) the cancers and toxins and germs that are already in your system - trying to flush them out of your body. The sunshine is one of God's 8 Natural Remedies!

V. TEMPERANCE

"In order to preserve health, temperance in all things is necessary - temperance in labor, temperance in eating and drinking." How to Live, pg. 57. (Ellen White).

"True temperance teaches us to dispense entirely with everything hurtful, and to use judiciously that which is healthful." The Faith I Live By, pg. 231. (Ellen White).

Many Christians believe that "Moderation" is the KEY. We strongly disagree. Think about it...is cocaine OK in moderation? Of course not! You see, True Temperance means to abstain completely from things that are bad for you and to use "moderately" those things that are good for you.

About a 100 years ago, there was something called - The Temperance Pledge . At that time, people who signed it were promising to not drink or have anything to do with liquor. It would be good if we could have a Temperance Pledge today. But, it should include way more than liquor. Our bodies are the "temple" of God. We should not put anything into it that is not good for it. Let's think about that for a moment. What are some common things that people put into their bodies that are not good for them? Coffee? Cigarette smoke? Chocolate? The vast majority of the Artificial Sweeteners? And what about all the Prescription Drugs so many people are on? The side-effects of many of them are horrendous!

If you feel a bit overwhelmed, and maybe discouraged...thinking about the things that need changing in your lifestyle, don't give up! Email us, tell us what you know you need to do, and we'll give you some suggestions as to how to do it successfully! We can help! And most of all, God is just waiting to help you, if you will only let Him. Come join us and be a Health Reformer! Sign the Temperance Pledge! You'll feel so much better.

VI. AIR

"Air is the free blessing of heaven, calculated to electrify the whole system." (Ellen White)

"Thousands have died for want of pure water and pure air, who might have lived...These blessings they need in order to become well. If they would become enlightened, and let medicine alone and accustom themselves to outdoor exercise, and to air in their houses, summer and winter, and use soft water for drinking and bathing purposes, they would be comparatively well and happy instead of dragging out a miserable existence." How to Live, pg. 56. (Ellen White)

Pure, clean air, is another one of God's 8 Natural Remedies

VII. REST

"I know that from the testimonies given me from time to time, for brain workers, that sleep is worth far more before than after midnight. Two hours good sleep before 12 o'clock is worth more than four hours after 12 o'clock...(Ellen White)

"Give yourself proper time to sleep. They who sleep give nature time to build up and repair the weary waste of the organs." (Ellen White).

"The number of hours of sleep generally needed varies with circumstances The average is seven to nine. In general one should sleep when sleepy and not try to sleep more. Growing children require more sleep than grown-ups." (Ellen White).

"Ones best sleep is with the stomach practically empty. It is true that food puts one to sleep at first, by diverting blood from the head; but it disturbs sleep later. Water, unless it induces bladder-action during the night, or even fruit, may be taken without injury before retiring. If one goes to bed with an empty stomach, he can often get along well with six or seven hours sleep, but if he goes to bed soon after a hearty meal, he usually needs from eight to ten hours sleep...It has already been pointed out that sleeping outdoors is more restful than sleeping indoors." How to Live, pg. 120-121. (Ellen White).

Many people, when they need rest , instead of going to sleep, drink coffee to stay awake. That is exactly the opposite of what they need. Coffee and ephedrine and energy pills cannot replace rest. Rest is also one of God's 8 Natural Remedies.

VIII. TRUST IN GOD

"Gratitude, rejoicing, benevolence, trust in God 's love and care -- these are health's greatest safeguards." My Life Today, pg. 151. (Ellen White).

"Not a few, in this Christian age and Christian nation, resort to mediums rather than trust to the power of the living God. The mother, watching by the sick-bed of her child, exclaims, "I can do no more. Is there no physician who has power to restore my child?" She is told of the wonderful cures performed by some clairvoyant or magnetic healer, and she trusts her dear one to his charge, placing it as verily in the hands of Satan as though he were standing by her side. And in how many instances is the future life of the child controlled by a Satanic power which it seems powerless to breath!" The Signs of the Times, March 24, 1887. (Ellen White).

Science has proven now, that people who trust in God , and have faith, come through illnesses and surgeries better than those who do not trust in God.

If you would like to learn "HOW" to trust in God , there is a booklet called "Steps to Christ" you can have for free.

Just visit the website <u>Steps to Christ</u> (http://mcdonald.southern.edu/bible/script/ teps/) or send me an <u>email</u> to alexandrinen@yahoo.com. Just mention that you would like the booklet - "*Steps to Christ*".

Appendix 1 taken from:
http://www.faculty.umb.edu/alexandrine_n oel/AlexINFO/newstart.htm

Appendix 2

Appendix 2 taken from:
 http://sdapillars.blogspot.com/p/gods-eight-laws-ofhealth-our-designers.html

SDA Pillars of Our Faith
 God's Eight Laws of Health
OUR DESIGNER'S PLAN FOR GLOWING HEALTH

"Beloved, I wish above all things that thou mayest prosper and be in health as thy soul prospereth." 3John 2

For glowing health, follow your Designer's hand-book; The BIBLE.

And God said, Behold, I have given you every herb bearing seed, which is upon the face of all the earth, and every tree, in the which is the fruit of a tree yielding seed; to you it shall be for meat. Gen.1.29

...and thou shalt eat the herb of the field; Gen.3.18

"For I know the thoughts that I think toward you, says the Lord, thoughts of peace and not of evil, to give you a future and a hope." Jer. 29:11

1. NUTRITION

2. EXERCISE

3. WATER

4. SUNSHINE

5.TEMPERANCE

6.AIR

7.REST

8. TRUST IN GOD

HOW DO WE KNOW THAT THIS IS GOD'S ONLY HEALTH PLAN?

Well, any plan for health that God would have would have to fill these following specifications:

It would have to have been available to all generations since creation

It could not be available only to people in the 20th century or only in developed countries. It could not involve any high technology.

It would have to be able to be done at home.

It would have to be able to be understood by all, educated or not educated. It must be 100% natural.

It must be Inexpensive so the poor could also use it. It would cause absolutely no harm to the body.

It would not depend on torturing and death of myriads of God's creatures to develop it. It would not require skilled personnel to administer it.

It would not use items so poisonous that a small error in dose is deadly. It would be available to all; not just a privileged few.

There is no other plan out there that meets all these requirements: This IS God's health program and He throws it out to you as a life-ring. Grab it and be blessed.

NUTRITION

THE HEALTHY DIET: Avoids all refined foods; Uses fruits, vegetables, nuts and seeds, legumes and grains, as fresh & simple as possible. Fresh is best, Frozen next best, dried is OK also. Eat as much as possible fresh & raw. Sprouts are very good. Reduce oil and fat, including margarine and vegetable oils and things made with them; especially Canola oil. (Read Labels)

Use no refined sugar; Aspartame or artificial sweeteners: replace with honey or dried fruits and use these lightly.

Avoid 'salt bombs' such as cheezies, chips, pretzels and party snacks. Most cheese is extremely high in fat & salt and should be limited.

Use no deep fried foods.

Don't mix fruits and vegetables at the same meal. Avoid 'hot' spices and vinegar.

Cook in Glass, stainless steel, or enamel, not aluminum. (or better still eat it raw) If you can, get organically grown foods.

Avoid micro waved, and irradiated produce.

A good rule is: "IF IT GROWS on plants, EAT IT; and EAT IT IN AS NATURAL A STATE AS POSSIBLE." The more man does with a food the less nutritional value it has left when he is finished.

EXERCISE

Begin a program of walking; walk as far as is comfortable, gradually working up to 3 or 4 miles a day. Take a walking stick for stability. Work up to a minimum of 20-30 minutes at least every other day. If muscles are weak, every other day is better, as it takes 48 hrs. recovery time.

Can't go out? A rebounder, (mini trampoline) is good for some. Organic Gardening is also great exercise for health. (and the side effect is yummy vegetables.)

WATER

Your body is about 75% water. Lots of water is needed for optimal function. Every process in your body depends on the presence of adequate water.

Drink lots of pure, soft water daily. Distilled or reverse osmosis water is best. Juice, tea or soft drinks do NOT take the place of water. Your weight ÷ 2= minimum number of oz. of water to drink daily. Adequate fluid intake will increase your endurance and energy levels. Studies show DEHYDRATION at the cellular level to be the root cause of many diseases. Carry a supply with you at work and on walks etc.

On arising squeeze a fresh lemon into two glasses room temperature or warm water and drink it. Drink between meals. 2 hours after to 1/2 hour before, not with meals. Taking 2 glasses 1/2 hour before each meal, prevents mealtime thirst, aids digestion and prevents ulcers. Shower daily with cool or tepid water using a bath brush or good rough washcloth to rub your skin all over. This improves circulation and helps the body to get toxins out.

SUNSHINE

Sunshine has several benefits to the body. It furnishes the natural Vitamin D and helps to lower cholesterol. Sunlight increases the volume of oxygen in the blood. Start with 10-15 minutes daily to face and hands and work up to 30-45 minutes daily. The best time for sunbathing is 9-10 am and 4-6 PM. Avoid burning. To lessen skin cancer risk, reduce the fat intake, such as animal fats, oils, margarine - (and foods containing refined, processed oils)

TEMPERANCE

Temperance is not only concerned with drinking booze or smoking; good health requires moderation and wise choices in all aspects of life. Over-eating, over-playing, over-working, and over-indulgence of the marriage privilege can all contribute to poor health. Abstain from all harmful indulgences; Tobacco, alcohol coffee, tea, (except herbal tea) colas and soft drinks. The bit of pleasure they might give is not worth the misery they cause in the long run.

AIR

Pure fresh air is very important to our well being. That means good air with lots of oxygen. Walking in forests and nature is great. Do some deep breathing exercises daily, this is very helpful in the morning. Even in winter have windows open a little and air rooms daily. Avoid smoke, chemicals, Room fresheners and aerosol sprays.

REST

Get adequate restful sleep; an early, light supper, well before bedtime and no eating before bed will help. A relaxing warm bath may help you unwind, avoid stressful and stimulating activities before bedtime. Regular times for going to bed and rising will also help. The best time to go to bed is between 9 and 10 PM. This sounds strange, because in our culture, it almost seems in bad taste to sleep. 100 years ago the average person got 9 or more hours sleep. Now it is more like 4 or 5. Exercise during the day also helps set the stage for restful sleep. Avoid using drugs for sleep, as these are harmful and sleep thus attained is of little benefit to your body. Lack of restful sleep is for many the root of the 'enervation' that brings disease. For healing and cleansing to occur much rest and sleep is needed as these actions are done only while asleep.

TRUST IN GOD

An abiding faith in our loving God will help you. He has made every provision to forgive and cleanse all our past mistakes. He will give power to break harmful addictions and help us overcome bitter and angry attitudes that 'eat us up' inside. If we are 'Willing to be made willing' He will work with us, take away our love for sinning and make us free in Him. Ask Him.

Have you ever really read the Bible?

Oh, I don't mean just looking up a text at church; I mean really read it as a letter of love from God to you personally?

Well, when you do, you will find it full of precious promises; each one meant for you just as much as anybody else.

Do you know what 'Faith' is? Well, it is simply taking God at His word; in other words, believing that He means what He says in His Word, the Bible. If you take time every day to read God's Word as personal to you and talk to Him about His promises; your life will blossom as you have never dreamed.

NUTRITION

"In the beginning God created the heaven and the earth" Genesis 1:1

Genesis 1:27 God created man. When formed, Adam and Eve were given "noble TRAITS of character" and "High intellectual powers," yet they were to develop character by the CHOICES they made.

Therefore, "at the very beginning of man's existence a check was placed upon the desire for self-indulgence," and "the tree of knowledge [food]...was to be a TEST of obedience, faith, and love of our first parents."

Genesis 2:17, Genesis 3:6

Death is mostly E-A-T. And Satan "overcame Adam and Eve upon appetite." For through "indulgence of appetite" Satan can control our "minds and being." If a person conquers appetite he will have the "moral power to gain the victory over EVERY other temptation of Satan". Inasmuch as "food" is a constant temptation right from birth, appetite is a very wonderful training tool. The baby's mother should present only a strict vegetarian diet (other than actual breast feeding), training the child to continually exercise self-control, remembering that its character is formed and its destiny determined by the CHOICES it makes.

Genesis 1:29, 30

The first chapters of the Bible, reveal that both man and animal were created to be strict vegetarians. (The only exception, apparently, was the nursing of offspring on its mother's milk, until weaning.) In other words, man was to exist upon natural foods, without even the use of dairy or egg products.

Blood and Fat

About 1700 years later, after the Flood had torn up the vegetation, God allowed (not commanded) men to eat flesh. But if they did, they would pay price, having their life span reduced by the very animals they ate. (Of the hundreds of animal diseases, it is known that more than half can be passed from animal to man.) The average life span of man before the Flood was about 909 years. But after animal and animal products were introduced into the diet, the next 10 generations lost an average of 73 years of life per generation, down to Abraham's age of 175 years. (And today, despite modern medicines, we are still down 70-75 years, which still does not recommend this type of diet.)

Several hundred years later, when God led His chosen people out of Egyptian slavery, He immediately switched them over to vegetarian manna. But they preferred flesh and eventually were allowed such, with regulations.

"Upon their settlement in Canaan, the Israelites were permitted the use of animal food, but under careful restrictions, which tended to lessen the evil results. The use of swine's flesh was prohibited, as also of other animals and of birds and fish whose flesh was pronounced unclean. Of the meats permitted, the eating of the fat and the blood was strictly forbidden." Testimony Studies on Diets & Food 63

Leviticus 3:17

"The Israelites were forbidden to eat the fat or the blood. 'It shall be a perpetual statute for your generations throughout all your dwellings, that ye eat neither fat nor blood This law not only related to beasts for sacrifice, but to all cattle which were used for food. This law was to impress upon them the important fact that if there had been no sin there would have been no shedding of blood...

"The blood of the Son of God was symbolized by the blood of the slain victim, and God would have clear and definite ideas preserved between the sacred and the common. Blood was sacred, inasmuch as through the shedding of the blood of the Son of God alone could there be atonement for sin. Blood was also used to cleanse the sanctuary from the sins of the people, thus typifying the blood of Christ which alone can cleanse from sin. The fat was to be used in sacrificial offerings with the beasts, but in no case was it a suitable article of food. If used, disease would be the sure result." ST 7/15/1880

Leviticus 7:25-27

"For whosoever eateth the fat of the beast, of which men offer an offering made by fire unto the Lord, even the soul that eateth it shall be cut off from his people. Moreover ye shall eat no manner of blood, whether it be of fowl or of beast, in any of your dwellings. Whatsoever soul it be that eateth any manner of blood, even that soul shall be cut off from his people." Isaiah 11:6-9; 65:21-25.

Again, through Isaiah, God pointed toward complete vegetarianism (Compare with Daniel 1:8- 16).

John the Baptist was a vegetarian picture of what God's people are to become in these last days (Mark 1:6, 7)

"Locusts" are pods of the Locust or Carob tree, and the Spirit of Prophecy confirms that John's diet was "purely vegetable"
Revelation 21:4

Likewise, John the Revelator spoke of a time when there would be "no more" pain or death

Genesis 1:29

"And God said, 'Behold, I have given you every herb bearing seed...and every tree in the which is the fruit of a tree yielding seed; to you it shall be for meat (food)."

Proverbs 21:9

[It is] better to dwell in a corner of the housetop, than with a brawling woman in a wide house.

Solomon recognized the effects of emotional stress on our well-being. Our attitude while eating is important. If we are nervous, or in a hurry or upset about something, the digestive process is impaired. It is better not to eat at all, unless we can do so in a positive frame of mind and take our time. Hurried eating tends to overeating. Since digestion begins in the mouth, it is important to chew your food well.

The Bible is full of references to honey and the honeycomb.

Proverbs 24:13; "My son, eat thou honey, because it is good; and the honeycomb which is sweet to thy taste"

Proverbs 25:16,27 "Hast thou found honey? eat so much as is sufficient for thee"

Proverbs 25:27 "It is not good to eat much honey"

Proverbs 16:24 "Pleasant words are as a honeycomb, sweet to the soul and health to the bones"

Protein

In the past, some people believed one could never get too much protein. In the early 1900s, Americans were told to eat well over 100 grams of protein a day. And as recently as the 1950s, health- conscious people were encouraged to boost their protein intake.

Recommended protein intake for men is 63 grams. The average protein consumed by a non-vegetarian man is 103 grams. The average protein consumed by a vegetarian man is 105 grams.

For women, the recommended protein intake for women is 50 grams. The average protein consumed by a non- vegetarian woman is 74 grams. And the average protein consumed by a vegetarian woman is 65 grams.

Obviously, there is no problem with vegetarians getting enough protein. If any problem exists, it is the other way around.

Excess protein consumption has been linked to many diseases.

Today, some fad diets encourage high-protein intake for weight loss, though Americans tend to take in nearly twice the amount of protein they need anyway. And while individuals following such a diet have had short-term success in losing weight, they are often unaware of the health risks associated with a high-protein diet. Excess protein has been linked with osteoporosis, kidney disease, calcium stones in the urinary tract, and some cancers.

Calcium in Plant-Based Diets

Many people choose to avoid milk because it contains fat, cholesterol, allergenic proteins, lactose sugar, and frequent traces of contamination, not to mention the health risks and the fact that 70% of dairy cows worldwide HAVE leukemia. Milk is also linked to juvenile- onset diabetes and other serious conditions.

The dairy industry has brain-washed us into thinking that we have to drink milk in order to get enough calcium. Happily, there are plenty of other good sources of calcium.

Keeping your bones strong depends more on preventing the loss of calcium from your body than on boosting your calcium intake. Some cultures consume no dairy products and typically ingest only 175 to 475 milligrams of calcium per day. However, these people generally have low rates of osteoporosis. Many scientists believe exercise and other factors have more to do with osteoporosis than calcium intake does.

Calcium in the Body

Almost all of the calcium in the body is in the bones. There is a tiny amount in the blood stream which is responsible for important functions such as muscle contraction, maintenance of the heartbeat, and transmission of nerve impulses.

We constantly lose calcium from our bloodstream through urine, sweat, and feces. It is renewed with calcium from bone. In this process, bones continuously lose calcium. This bone calcium must be replaced from food.

Calcium needs change throughout life. Up until the age of 30 or so, we consume more calcium than we lose.

Adequate calcium intake during childhood and adolescence is especially important. Later, the body begins to slip into "negative calcium balance," and the bones start to lose more calcium than they take up. The loss of too much calcium can lead to soft bones or osteoporosis.

How rapidly calcium is lost depends, in part, on the kind and amount of protein you eat as well as other diet and lifestyle choices.

Reducing Calcium Loss

A number of factors affect calcium loss from the body:

•Diets that are high in protein cause more calcium to be lost through the urine. Protein from animal products is much more likely to cause calcium loss than protein from plant foods. This may be one reason that vegetarians tend to have stronger bones than meat eaters.

•Caffeine increases the rate at which calcium is lost through urine.

•Drinking soda pop is reported to leech calcium from the body.

•Diets high in sodium increase calcium losses in the urine.

•Alcohol inhibits calcium absorption.

•The mineral boron may slow the loss of calcium from bones.

•Exercise slows bone loss and is one of the most important factors in maintaining bone health.

Cooking without Eggs

Many people choose not to use eggs in their diet. About 70 percent of the calories in eggs are from fat, and a big portion of that fat is saturated. They are also loaded with cholesterol -- about 213 milligrams for an average-sized egg. Because egg shells are fragile and porous and conditions on egg farms are crowded, eggs are the perfect host to salmonella-the bacteria that is the leading cause of food poisoning in this country.

Eggs are often used in baked products because of their binding and leavening properties. But smart cooks have found good substitutes for eggs. Try one of the following the next time you prepare a recipe that calls for eggs:

If a recipe calls for just one or two eggs, you can often skip them. Add a couple of extra tablespoons of water for each egg eliminated to balance out the moisture content of the product.

Eggless egg replacers are available in many natural food stores. These are different from reduced-cholesterol egg products which do contain eggs. Egg replacers are egg-free and are usually in a powdered form. Replace eggs in baking with a mixture of the powdered egg replacer and water according to package directions.

•Use 1 heaping tablespoon of soy flour or cornstarch plus 2 table-spoons of water to replace each egg in a baked product.

•Use 1 ounce of mashed tofu in place of an egg.

•In muffins and cookies, half of a mashed banana can be used instead of an egg, although it will change the flavor of the recipe somewhat.

•For vegetarian loaves and burgers, use any of the following to bind ingredients together: tomato paste, mashed potato, moistened bread crumbs, or rolled oats.

A good variety of plain, unrefined plant food is more nutritionally balanced than the animal products and man-made processed foods. Whole grains, fruits, vegetables, beans, peas, nuts and seeds contain high quality protein, a better fatty-acid profile (thus decreasing the risk of heart disease and cancer), no cholesterol, plenty of complex carbohydrates and fiber, and are rich in vitamins and minerals and water.

Animal products and man-made foods are often high in fat, cholesterol, sugar, salt, and harmful additives, and are lacking in fiber.

The chief concern then should be "What are the best sources available to me to get the nutrients I need?" We now know the answer to that question, "A well-balanced vegetarian diet that includes a variety of fruits, vegetables, whole grains, legumes, nuts, and seeds."

Vit B12 is often sighted as a problem in vegetarian diets but there are, contrary to popular opinion, many sources of non-animal B12. Sea vegetables, spirulina and other algae, turnip greens, tempeh, and sprouts for example. Also B12 is carefully hoarded by the body and a small supply last for many years. Pernicious anemia is, in most cases, caused by problems of absorption not supply and is found in meat eaters more often than vegetarians.

Also, any grain eaten with any legume gives you complete protein building blocks and so is very simple to use.

As serious disease in animals is rapidly increasing and has been shown to be passed to humans in the food chain, the safety of using any animal product is to be seriously questioned. Most of us know at least bits and pieces of the mad-cow saga still dragging on in England. There is strong evidence that the

British practice of feeding rendered scrapie-infected sheep to cows was the cause. With such recycling so commonplace in the United States, widespread concern is mounting.

VINEGAR, PEPPER & SPICES

These items should be eliminated from a healthful diet. Vinegar and Pepper both contribute to sclerosis of the liver and are worse even than alcohol to cause this problem. Even as little as 1/4 of a teaspoon of vinegar, interferes with digestion of a meal, causing food to ferment and foul the bloodstream with toxic waste products. Healthy, raw foods can be rendered useless to the body by addition of such things. Spices irritate digestive tract and cause nervousness and irritability. Salt should not be eliminated but used with great moderation All of these things are addictive and can be a battle to stop but learning to relish simple foods prepared without harmful condiments is worth the effort.

FAT FACTS

This statement from the World Health Organization's Executive Board in 1969 is very revealing:

Coronary heart disease (CHD) has reached enormous proportions, striking more and more at younger subjects. It will result in coming years in the greatest epidemic mankind has faced unless we are able to reverse the trend by concentrated research into its cause and prevention.

What are the greatest risk factors in CHD?

• diet high in saturated (solid) fats

• high blood lipids (cholesterol and triglycerides)

• family history of CHD in early life (prior to age 50)

• high blood pressure

- cigarette smoking

- obesity

- diabetes mellitus

- sedentary living

As God designed, in nature there is an abundance of natural fats available in nuts, seeds, avocado, vegetables and grains. Our bodies were designed to subsist on a low fat diet. When extra fats and free oils are added to the diet, not unlike other highly specialized machinery, the system begins to clog up.

Digestion of free oils and fats takes much longer than the digestion of other foods. A raw salad can be digested within two to three hours. When salad oils, such as corn, sesame, peanut, or other vegetable free fats are added to the salad, digestion is delayed for another two or three hours. When our food is coated with free oils the natural digestive processes are inhibited by preventing digestive juices access to these foods until the oils are digested -- consequently, by the time the fats and oils are digested, the elementary carbohydrates or proteins in the vegetables have begun to ferment.

"The salads are prepared with oil and vinegar, fermentation takes place in the stomach, and the food does not digest, but decays or putrefies; as a consequence, the blood is not nourished, but becomes filled with impurities, and liver and kidney difficulties appear."CDF

Ecclesiastes 10:17

"Blessed art thou, O land, when . . . thy princes eat in due season, for strength, and not for drunkenness."

Psalm 103:2-5
"Bless the LORD, O my soul, and forget not all his benefits: Who forgiveth all thine iniquities; who healeth all thy diseases; Who

redeemeth thy life from destruction; who crowneth thee with lovingkindness and tender mercies; Who satisfieth thy mouth with good [things; so that] thy youth is renewed like the eagle's."

Diet Facts in the U.S.

62% of Americans are overweight.

44 million Americans are considered clinically obese. Over half the nation is dieting or has dieted.

In 1982, 15 billion dollars were spent on weight-loss schemes.

Diets do not work. If they did, why is obesity increasing and new diets constantly being developed?

Statistics on Diet and Disease

1961--Journal of American Medical Association reported that a vegetarian diet can prevent 90- 97% of heart disease.

1977--In the Senate Report on Nutrition and Human Needs, Dr. Mark Hegsted of the Harvard

School of Public Health said:

"I wish to stress that there is a great deal of evidence, and it continues to accumulate, which strongly implicates, and in some instances, proves that the major causes of death and disability in the United States are related to the diet we eat. I include coronary artery disease, which accounts for nearly half of the deaths in the United States, several of the most important forms of cancer, hypertension, diabetes, and obesity, as well as other chronic diseases."

1982--At the National Cancer Institute, doctors said, "Changing the way we eat could offer some protection against cancer." NCI has now made diet its number one area of research in cancer prevention.

1983--American Cancer Society stated its belief that "a greater use of fruit and vegetables can significantly reduce a person's risk of developing cancer."

Animal Disease Is On the Increase

Over 100 million chickens die per year of chicken leukemia. About 235 million chickens die each year from all causes - many of which are transmittable to humans. Yearbook of Agriculture, pp. 466-474.

Approximately 2 1/2 million beef livers are rejected annually by federal meat inspectors because they have cancer, abscesses or parasitic worms. The rest of the carcass is, however, allowed to be sold for human food. Yearbook of Agriculture, p. 11.

Approximately 40 million hogs and piglets die of disease on our farms each year and never (we hope) reach the meat market. About 3 1/4 million that do reach the slaughter house are rejected in part or total by meat inspectors. Life and Health, Oct. 1969, p. 31.

Over 71 thousand cattle were sold for human food in 1967 after malignant eye tumors were discovered. (Only the eye itself was condemned). Life and Health, Oct. 1969, p. 31.

Thousands of chickens contaminated or stained with feces are shipped every day instead of being condemned, 81 federal testified. The Atlanta Constitution, May 26, 1991.

In January 1993, contaminated hamburgers were the cause of the biggest outbreak ever of the deadly bacteria, E. Coli 0157:H7. The outbreak killed four children and hospitalized 500 people. The Spokesman Review, January 23, 1993.

In 1993 the USDA temporarily closed 30 beef slaughterhouses after inspections revealed contaminated carcasses at dozens of plants. The Tallahassee Democrat, May 28, 1993, p. 31.

Two cattle diseases, Bovine Immuno-deficiency Virus (cow AIDS) and Bovine Leukemia Virus have been discovered in the U.S. - BIV and BLV are widespread and suspected of being transmitted to humans through the ingestion pathway. Beyond Beef, Jeremy Rifkin, p. 143.

Animal Agriculture and Environmental Damage

Nearly 40% of the world's grain and nearly 70% of U.S. grain are fed to livestock.

Almost 1/2 of the energy used in American agriculture goes into livestock production. It takes the equivalent of 50 gallons of gasoline to produce the red meat and poultry eaten by the typical American each year - and twice that much to process, package, transport, sell, store and cook it.

Livestock agriculture takes nearly 1/3 of California irrigation water, which amounts to about 190 gallons of water per meat-eating

American per day - twice the daily water usage in the average American home.

Half of the continental United States is used for feedstock, pasture, and range. Half of U.S. cropland grows animal feed and hay. This land is eroding quickly. For each pound of red meat, poultry, eggs and milk, farm fields lose five pounds of prime topsoil.

270 million acres of public land in the western United States are leased to ranchers for grazing.

Already, 10% of this land has been turned into desert by livestock; 70% is severely degraded.

Livestock produces 158 million tons of waste per year, some of which contaminates underground water tables with nitrates. Animal waste and feed fertilizers account for 40% of the phosphorous released into American rivers, lakes and streams.

The Vegetarian Times, Ot. 1991, p. 68.

EXERCISE

AND the LORD God took the man (Adam], and put him into the garden of Eden to dress it and to keep it." Genesis 2:15.

God's original plan was for people to be active. Physical activity is necessary to maintain all our functional body units and to keep a reserve physical capacity to handle emergency situations.

"God designed that the living machinery should be in daily activity. For in this activity or motion is its preserving power.... The more we exercise, the better will be the circulation of the blood." -- Ellen G. White, Healthful Living, pp. 131-132

"There is no exercise that can take the place of walking. By it the circulation of the blood is greatly improved. Walking, in all cases where it is possible, is the best remedy for the diseased bodies, because in this, all of

the organs of the body are brought into use."
-- Ellen G. White, Testimonies, Vol. 3, p. 78

"Moderate exercise every day will impart strength to the muscles, which without exercise become flabby and enfeebled." -- Ellen G. White, Testimonies, Vol. 2, p. 533

"Exercise will aid in the work of digestion. Take a walk after a meal; but no violent exercise after a full meal." -- Ellen G. White, Testimonies, Vol. 2, p. 530

"Morning exercise, walking in the free, invigorating air of heaven, or cultivating flowers, small fruits, and vegetables, is the surest safeguard against colds, coughs, congestion of the brain, inflammation of the liver, the kidneys, and the lungs, and a hundred other diseases." -- Ellen G. White, Healthful Living, p. 176-177

"If physical exercise were combined with mental exertion, the blood would be quickened in its circulation, the action of the heart would be more perfect, impure matter would be thrown off, and new life and vigor would be experienced in every part of the body." -- Ellen G. White, Counsels on Health, p. 572

"Those who thus exercise the Christian graces will grow and will become strong to work for God. They will have a clear spiritual perceptions, a steady growing faith, and an increased power in prayer.... Strength comes by exercise. Activity is the very condition of life. Those who endeavor to maintain a Christian life by passively accepting the blessing that come through the means of grace, and doing nothing for Christ, are simply trying to live by eating without working.... A man who would refuse to exercise his limbs would soon lose all power to use them. Thus the Christian who will not exercise his God-given powers, not only fails to grow up into Christ, but he loses the strength that he already had." -- Ellen G. White, Steps to Christ, p. 80

Leviticus 17:11

"The life of the flesh is in the blood." What is in the blood constitutes life; and if there is life in the blood, but bad circulation, the entire system cannot receive the life it needs. Each cell in the body requires nourishment and cleansing from its own wastes to be healthy. Nutrients are delivered to each cell through the blood stream, and, in turn, the wastes are picked up and deposited in the eliminating organs. Thus we can understand the statement, "Perfect health depends upon perfect circulation." (2T 531).

"The more active the circulation, the more free from obstructions and impurities will be the blood." (Healthful Living, p. 178).

The very best exercise is walking briskly outdoors.

"There is NO exercise that can take the place of walking. By it the circulation of the blood is greatly improved. Walking, in all cases where it is possible, is the best remedy for diseased bodies, because in this exercise all the organs of the body are brought into use." (3T 78).

"There is no exercise that will prove as beneficial to every part of the body as walking."
(Healthful Living, p. 130).

I will praise thee; for I am fearfully and wonderfully made; marvelous are thy works; and that my soul knoweth right well." Psalms 139:14

Cells need four essential things to live and function properly:

OXYGEN: Without oxygen, cells die within three minutes; pure air brings life to the skin; for a lack of air the skin nearly dies;

WATER: Without water, the cells die in a few days;

NUTRITION: Without nutrients they die in a few weeks;

CLEANSING: Their own wastes must be removed promptly or death will result in a matter of minutes, or at the most a matter of hours "The studied habit of shunning the air and avoiding exercise, closes the pores, the little mouths through which the body breathes, making it impossible to throw off impurities through that channel. The burden of labor is throne upon the lungs, kidneys, etc., and these internal organs are compelled to do the work of the skin." 2T 524

1 Timothy 4:8 "For bodily exercise profiteth little: but godliness is profitable unto all things, having promise of the life that now is, and of that which is to come."

In this text we would almost think the apostle is telling us not to exercise but that is not what is being said.

He is telling us that developing our bodies is not to be more important to us than learning to follow and obey God. You see, Paul lived at the time when the Greek Olympic contests were considered so important. The Pagans worshiped the human body and often put everything into athletic training. It was their idol, so to speak.

And so we must be careful because it is easy to make sports, athletics, games of skill, or physical training an idol, to the neglect of our souls and the service of God.

Genesis 3:17- 19 "And unto Adam he said, Because thou hast hearkened unto the voice of thy wife, and hast eaten of the tree, of which I commanded thee, saying, Thou shalt not eat of it: cursed [is] the ground for thy sake; in sorrow shalt thou eat [of] it all the days of thy life; Thorns also and thistles shall it bring forth to thee; and thou shalt eat the herb of the field; In the sweat of thy face shalt thou eat bread, till thou return unto the ground; for out of it wast thou taken: for dust thou [art], and unto dust shalt thou return."

It is often said; Oh how terrible that God cursed the earth, but you will notice it said, 'for your sake' God wasn't 'getting even' as it were, He was making things so that man would have to work hard to live as that is the only way he would stay strong and well in a sinful world. God's plan for mans physical prosperity is not sports and games, but rather practical, worthwhile work. God's blessing is on those who follow His wise plan and they get more pleasure and satisfaction from life than the idle person ever does.

Proverbs 13:4 "The soul of the sluggard desireth, and [hath] nothing: but the soul of the diligent shall be made fat."

Proverbs 20:4 "The sluggard will not plow by reason of the cold; [therefore] shall he beg in harvest, and [have] nothing."

Proverbs 6:9 "How long wilt thou sleep, O sluggard? when wilt thou arise out of thy sleep?"

Proverbs 22:29 "Seest thou a man diligent in his business? he shall stand before kings; he shall not stand before mean [men]".

Proverbs 22:29 "Seest thou a man diligent in his business? he shall stand before kings; he shall not stand before mean [men]."

Ecclesiastes 5:12 "The sleep of a labouring man [is] sweet, whether he eat little or much: but the abundance of the rich will not suffer him to sleep."

Yes, God means us to use the physical abilities He has given us and also use simple exercise to stay fit, but Sports and Athletics can be a snare and become an Idol and are not God's way. These things lead to PRIDE, and take our minds from heavenly things it is no help to have a strong body and loose your own soul.

Matthew 16:26 "For what is a man profited, if he shall gain the whole world, and lose his own soul?or what shall a man give in exchange for his soul?"

Working, outdoors especially, and walking in nature are two excellent ways to stay in shape as they allow us to contemplate the works of God and meditate on Him, they do not cost a lot to do them, and they do not engender pride and competitive attitudes.

WATER

Genesis 2:10

"And a river went out of Eden and watered the garden."

John 4:14

"But whosoever drinketh of the water that I shall give him shall never thirst; but the water that I shall give him shall be in him a well of water springing up into everlasting life."

Notice Jesus equates Himself and His truth with Water; the water of life.

John 6:35 "And Jesus said unto them, I am the bread of life: he that cometh to me shall never hunger; and he that believeth on me shall never thirst."

Jesus is the one who cleanses us from sin within and without.- another function of water. And just as it is necessary to our physical life for each cell to be washed clean of impurities, so it is necessary if we are to have eternal life that every part of our minds and hearts must be surrendered to Jesus to be cleansed of sin by His blood.

"Water is the best liquid possible to cleanse the tissues.... Drink some, a little time before or after a meal." -- Ellen G. White, Healthful Living, p. 226

Thought- how far would you get if you tried to wash your dirty clothes in pop? Or other drinks?

"The bath soothes the nerves. It promotes general perspiration, quickens the circulation, overcomes obstruction in the system, and acts beneficially on the kidneys and the urinary organs. Bathing helps the bowels, stomach, and liver, giving energy and new life to each. It also promotes digestion and instead of the system being weakened, it is strengthened...and a more easy and regular flow of the blood through all the blood vessels is obtained." -- Ellen G. White, Counsels on Health, p. 104

"Impurities are constantly and imperceptibly passing from the body, through the pores, and if the surface of the skin is not kept in a healthy condition, the system is burdened with impure matter....and if the garments worn are not frequently cleansed...the pores of the skin absorb again the waste matter thrown off. The impurities of the body... are taken back into the blood, and forced upon the internal organs." -- Ellen G. White, Healthful Living, p. 143

"God is the source of life and light and joy to the universe. Like rays of light from the sun, like the streams of living water bursting from a living spring, blessings flow out from Him to all His creatures. And wherever the life of God is in the hearts of men, it will flow out to others in love and

147

blessing." -- Ellen G. White, Steps to Christ, p. 77

Exodus 19:10

"And the LORD said unto Moses, Go unto the people, and sanctify them today and tomorrow, and let them wash their clothes," The saying, 'Cleanliness is next to godliness' is not in the Bible, but if you read the careful instruction given to the children of Israel by the Lord in regard to cleanliness of person, clothing, and surroundings, you will clearly see that hygienic practices of cleanliness and order will truly be followed by anyone who is obedient to God. To appear before God in dirty garments or with dirty bodies in an offense also when we realize that we have the holy angels with us when we belong to Jesus, and they come from heaven where all is clean and orderly, we will want to do our best to have this in our own surroundings as well.

Revelation 22:1

"And he showed me a pure river of water of life, clear as crystal, proceeding out of the throne of God and of the Lamb."

Can you even imagine what that water is going to be like? None of us have any idea how wonderful it will be. I once read about when the first white explorers found the Great Lakes that the water was crystal clear and you could see down to great depths in it, we can't even imagine That let alone what water in heaven and the New Earth will be like.

SOME OTHER SPIRITUAL LESSONS FROM WATER

Jesus likens Himself to the 'Water of Life'. There are many things we can learn from this comparison. Water is cleansing; Jesus cleanses us from sin. Water is essential to life; Jesus is essential for eternal life. Water always seeks the lowest place; it cheerfully and without complaint, quickly goes to the 'lowest room'. Jesus is the meek and lowly One; He is the humble God, who came down to the very depths to reach His fallen children.

Philippians 2:8 "And being found in fashion as a man, he humbled himself, and became obedient unto death, even the death of the cross." When we are imbued with His spirit, we will never be found seeking the highest place, but like the water, singing with joy we will seek the way of lowly service.

If you have every sat beside a sparking, splashing stream, you have seen another spiritual lesson from water. When flowing over rocks and rough places, water sings joyously. So may we rejoice in tribulations, and as water surely wears away and smoothes rough and jagged rocks, so does Jesus' grace in our lives smooth the path we must travel with peace and joy.

When you are near flowing water in a falls or fountain, this singing, joyous water seeking the lowest place, imparts an invigorating, refreshing atmosphere to all around it. So the life of Jesus, and his true children filled with His Spirit, has a heavenly and refreshing effect on all around that do not harden their hearts to this blessing.

Your body is about 75% water. Lots of water is needed for optimal function. Every process in your body depends on the presence of adequate water.

Drink lots of pure, soft water daily. Distilled water is best. Juice, tea or soft drinks do NOT take the place of water. Your weight.÷ 2= minimum number of oz. of water to drink daily. Adequate fluid intake will increase your endurance and energy levels. Studies show DEHYDRATION at the cellular level to be the root cause of many diseases. Carry a supply with you at work and on walks etc.

On arising squeeze a fresh lemon into two glasses room temperature or hot water and drink it.

A couple large glasses of hot water first thing in the morning will assist your bowels in elimination.

Drink between meals. 2 hours after to 1/2 hour before- not with meals. Taking 2 glasses 1/2 hour before each meal, prevents mealtime thirst, aids digestion and prevents ulcers. Shower daily with cool or tepid water using a bath brush or good rough washcloth to rub your skin all over. This improves circulation and gets toxins out. Food should not be washed down, and no drink is needed with meals. Many make a mistake in drinking cold water with their meals.

Taken with meals, water diminishes the flow of the salivary glands, and the colder the water, the greater the injury to the stomach. Eat slowly and allow the saliva to mingle with the food. The more liquid there is taken into the stomach with the meals, the more difficult it is for the food to digest, for the liquid must first be absorbed Other benefits of water are hydrotherapy, hot and cold fomentation, enemas, etc.

152

There are a lot of opinions on the go about what water is best for our health. The authorities fill our water with poisonous chemicals and assure us it is healthy to drink, mineral water sellers hold up their product and say it is best, Water bottlers sell us spring water. Well, we will give you some facts that I am sure will solve the problem for you and start you on your way to better health.

COMMON SENSE REASONS WHY YOU SHOULD DRINK PURE, DISTILLED WATER.

♦There are over 12,000 chemicals on the market today, 500 more being added yearly.

Regardless of where you live, in the city or on the farm, some of these chemicals are getting into your drinking water.

♦ No one on the face of the earth today, knows what effect these chemicals can have, as they go into thousands of different combinations. It is like mixing colors, one drop can change the whole shade.

◆There has not been equipment designed to detect many of these chemicals.

◆The body is made of 65% water. Therefore, don't you think you should be particular about the kind of water you drink?

◆ The Navy has been drinking distilled water for several generations.

◆ Distilled water is chemical and mineral free. Distillation removes the chemicals and impurities from water that are possible to remove, and if distillation doesn't remove them, there is no known method that will.

◆Our body does need minerals. HOWEVER- our body can only use organic minerals. That is minerals from plant or animal source. We cannot use inorganic minerals- only plants can use inorganic minerals. All those nice sounding minerals listed on your mineral water bottle are only able to be used by plants. That's right- they are totally unavailable to your body. What do

154

they do in there? They clog it up, making deposits in joints, stones in kidneys and gallbladders, rock-like plaque lining our arteries, making them hard and easy to break, leading to strokes and senility. Want your minerals? Dump your mineral water on your plants and then eat their fruit- it's the only way you get it.

♦ Distilled water is used for intravenous feedings, inhalation therapy, prescriptions, and baby formulas. Doesn't it make sense that it is good for everyone?

♦ Thousands of distillers have been sold to individuals, families, doctors, clinics, hospitals, government agencies and nursing homes. And these informed and alert consumers are helping protect their health, by using pure distilled water.

♦With all of the pollutants and impurities in our water, doesn't it only make sense to clean up the water you drink, the inexpensive way, through distillation- Nature's way of purifying water.

Inorganic minerals do nothing but harm in our bodies. People who live in areas where the water contains high levels of minerals find their arteries and veins get hard like cement as they age.

Chlorine and fluorine are two deadly poisons that the authorities see fit to lace our water with on a regular basis. Both these have been shown to contribute to cancer and disease.

SUNSHINE

AND God said, Let there be lights in the firmament of the heaven to divide the day from the night; and let them be for signs, and for seasons, and for days, and years: and let them be for lights in the firmament of the heaven to give light upon the earth: and it was so. And God made two great lights; the greater light to rule the day, and the lesser light to rule the night: he made the stars also. And God set them in the firmament of the heaven to give light upon the earth, and

156

to rule over the day and over the night, and to divide the light from the darkness: and God saw that it was good. And the evening and the morning were the fourth day." Genesis 1:14-19

Every living thing in our world is dependent on sunlight. Without sunlight nothing would live.

The following discoveries show the benefits derived from the sun: It lowers blood sugar and blood pressure; it lowers cholesterol by converting it to vitamin D; it utilizes calcium and phosphorus; it increases red blood cells; it increases white blood cells; it strengthens the immune system; it calms the nerves and increases adrenaline; it destroys germs on the skin; it reverses jaundice; it increases circulation; and it helps eliminate pesticides and other chemicals from the system.

Ecclesiastes 11:7 "Truly the light is sweet, and it is pleasant for the eyes to behold the sun"

"Pure air, good water, sunshine, the beautiful surroundings of nature...these are God's means for restoring the sick to health." -- Ellen G. White, Testimonies, Vol. 7, p. 85

"As the flower turns to the sun, that the bright beams may aid in perfecting its beauty and symmetry, so should we turn to the Sun of Righteousness, that Heaven's light may shine upon us, that our character may be developed in to the likeness of Christ." -- Ellen G. White, Steps to Christ, p. 68

Almost all of the food we eat depends upon sunlight to grow. In fact, the energy our bodies receive from the food we eat is, in a sense, solar energy that the plant has stored in the form of fats, carbohydrates, and proteins.

The ultraviolet rays are antiseptic and are capable of killing bacteria, viruses, fungi, yeasts, molds, and mites in air and water, and on surfaces. Even reflected light from north windows can destroy bacteria in the dust on window sills and floors. Since most window glass filters about 95 per cent of the ultraviolet rays, it would be well if they could be opened and the curtains pulled back for a period of time each day. Ultraviolet light also kills germs on our skin. This makes sunbathing a useful treatment for many skin diseases, such as diaper rash, athlete's foot, psoriasis, acne, boils, or impetigo.

Sunlight also toughens and thickens the skin, making it less susceptible to injury and infection.

Regular, controlled, moderate exposure to sunlight, instead of damaging the skin and aging it, actually protects the skin by building up a natural resistance to the harmful effects of ultraviolet light, while giving it a nice velvety texture. Later on we will discuss some precautions, but first, more benefits.

Ultraviolet light converts cholesterol in the skin to vitamin D. This vitamin is essential for the proper handling of calcium in the body and thus in the prevention of rickets and adult osteomalacia. Vitamin D is also added to some of the food we eat. It might be possible to get too much of the vitamin this way; but not when we get it from sunlight, since the body makes only what we need. Getting out in the sun, therefore, is a good way to lower cholesterol levels in our bodies. If we expose six square inches of our skin to direct sunlight for one hour per day, we will obtain our minimum daily requirement for vitamin D.

Sunlight helps to regulate almost all our bodily processes. Starting from the top (our minds) and working down, sunlight has been shown to increase our sense of well-being and to improve sleep. Ultraviolet light coming into our eyes stimulates the pineal gland, which helps to regulate our activity cycles. It has been said, "Dark nights and bright days will help keep the hormones in the body functioning properly." In one experiment hyperactivity in school children was decreased when the classroom's fluorescent lights were changed to full spectrum lighting. Thyroid function may improve. Hormone imbalances tend to level out.

Resting heart rate, blood pressure, and respiration rates are all decreased after a sunbath. This result is especially true if any of them were high to begin with. Blood sugar levels can be stabilized. (Note: Diabetics must use extra caution in the sun, as they are at greater risk of permanent injury from sunburn.)

Sunlight stimulates the production of more red blood cells, increasing the oxygen content of the blood, and thus increasing muscular endurance. It also stimulates production of more white blood cells and enhances oxygen utilization, which helps the body maintain its defense against disease. While certain skin cancers are associated with exposure to sunlight, the incidence of some of the more serious internal cancers seems to decrease.

Appetite may be improved, along with our assimilation, elimination, and metabolic processes.

Poisonous chemicals and heavy metals are removed from the bloodstream faster, while levels of healthy trace minerals are actually increased in the blood. Muscular strength has been increased, even in those unable to exercise. Sunlight has even been found helpful in the treatment of stomach ulcers.

As with most good things, there are some precautions to consider. The main concern is that of burning the skin. Normally, invisible pigment in the inner layer of the skin is converted to melanin, a much darker pigment that tends to reflect the sun's rays. But this process takes time.

Blue-eyed blondes and red-haired people are not as adept at this, and these are the very ones who tend to burn easiest. The amount of natural pigment in the skin is the most important factor.

For this reason Blacks have only about 20 percent as much skin cancer as Whites. For this same reason they also have more rickets, due to a lessened vitamin D production.

The amount of tan acquired from previous exposure is a factor, too. A good tan may screen out up to 90 percent of the burning rays. Also, there are persons who for some reason are supersensitive to even a brief exposure to the sun. Some drugs, deodorants, soaps, cosmetics, and beverage alcohol can sensitize the skin to sunlight, making it more sensitive.

FATS, OILS, AND SUNSHINE

You have no doubt heard the propaganda that sunshine is harmful and can cause cancer. Well it is partly true, but if our diets were free from unnatural fats, we would find cancer of the skin to be very rare indeed.

You see it is the action of the sun on all these TRANS fatty acids and hydrogenated fats in our skin that causes the mutations that lead to skin cancer.

Eliminate fried foods; (learn better ways to cook and you won't miss them) eliminate vegetable oils, and shortenings, margarine, and foods containing them. You will be surprised to find out that if you were a person who sunburns easily, after a while you will be no longer.

Toxic Oils Cotton seed oil, due to high amount of pesticides present in the crop, but also contains toxic fatty acids.

Canola, Rape and Mustard seed oils contain toxic fatty acids and there is oil called bromilated oil used in bottled fruit juices to prevent 'ring around the collar'. These are not listed on the label and are very toxic. The use of these is outlawed in some countries and they are harmful to thyroid, heart, kidney and liver. Peanut oil is best avoided as well.

Saturated fats like butter are less harmful as the body can use them fairly easily for fuel but even they should be used sparingly. Animal fats have the additional problem of contamination with pesticide, disease factors and chemical residues from the animal. The actual fat on meat was always forbidden to be used for food in the Bible. When referring to animal fat, I mean butter.

If you use a lot of processed and pre-prepared foods, you will not be able to eliminate a lot of harmful fats and oils so it is better to learn to prepare simple, fresh foods yourself so you know what you are eating. Better yet, eat as much as you can raw. For 'Fast Foods' you can't beat raw fruit.

For details on this subject, read the book: 'Fats and Oils' by Udo Erasmus.

An abundance of fruits, vegetables, and whole grains in the diet provides substances that help to prevent the formation of free radicals and protect against their harmful effects, and are thus important in order for the body to properly handle exposure to sunlight.

Overheating can lead to heat exhaustion or sunstroke. How can we best use sunlight to obtain the benefits while minimizing the risks? The first rule is tan, don't burn. Take into consideration the time of year and the hour of the day. As the sun moves more directly overhead, its intensity increases.

When sunbathing, unaccustomed persons should plan their exposures, keeping them short at first (2 minutes per side) and gradually increasing the duration and frequency of exposure. Any color change in the skin beyond the slightly pink stage is a sign you have overdone it.

The therapeutic effects occur just below the level of turning red. Remember that it takes time for skin color to change. Get out of the sun before you turn pink. If you don't, it may be too late. Also the benefits are enhanced with shorter, more frequent exposures.

When you've decided that you have had enough sun, the best sunscreen to wear is clothing.

Creams or oils are not necessary when sunbathing. Clean, dry skin is best for sunbathing.

Opaque ointments like zinc oxide are the best for total blockage to susceptible areas like the nose, and they do not wash off in water like other screens that usually need to be reapplied.

A helpful motto to remember when sunbathing is "Not too much, as often as possible."

Combine productive exercise in the fresh air and sunshine for a really healthful trio.

The Scriptures declare, "'Truly the light is sweet, and a pleasant thing it is for the eyes to behold the sun." Ecclesiastes 11:7

Our Saviour, God's Son, can be compared with the sun and all of its benefits. As we see the sun in the sky above, let us also remember that "unto you that fear my name shall the Sun of righteousness arise with healing in his wings." Malachi 4:2

TEMPERANCE

Genesis 2:9

"Out of the ground made the Lord God to grow every tree that is...good for food."

True temperance teaches us to dispense entirely with everything harmful and to use judiciously that which is healthful.

Temperance is not only concerned with drinking booze; good health requires moderation and wise choices in all aspects of life. Over-eating, over-playing, over-working, and over-indulgence of the marriage privilege can all contribute to poor health. Abstain from all harmful indulgences. Tobacco,
168

alcohol, colas and soft drinks, overeating, eating between meals, sugar- laden foods, strong condiments and spices, all caffeinated foods (chocolates and some sodas contain caffeine, as do coffee and tea), large combinations of foods, grease and fat, excess salt, and animal foods. The bit of pleasure they might give is not worth the misery they cause in the long run.

"Indulgence in eating too frequently, and in too large quantities, overtaxes the digestive organs, and produces a feverish state of the system. The blood becomes impure, and then diseases of various kinds occur." -- Review and Herald, September 5, 1899

"Abstemiousness in diet and control of the passions, will preserve the intellect and give mental and moral vigor, enabling men to bring all their propensities under the control of the higher powers, and to discern between right and wrong, the sacred and the common." -- Ellen G. White, Testimonies, Vol. 3, p. 491

Romans 12:1, 2

"I beseech you therefore, brethren, by the mercies of God, that ye present your bodies a living sacrifice, holy, acceptable unto God, which is your reasonable service. And be not conformed to this world: but be ye transformed by the renewing of your mind, that ye may prove what is that good, and acceptable, and perfect, will of God."

1 Corinthians 6.19, 20 "What? know ye not that your body is the temple of the Holy Ghost which is in you, which ye have of God, and ye are not your own? For ye are bought with a price: therefore glorify God in your body, and in your spirit, which are God's."

AND the LORD God commanded the man, saying, Of every tree of the garden thou mayest freely eat: but of the tree of the knowledge of good and evil, thou shalt not eat of it: for in the day that thou eatest thereof thou shalt surely die." Genesis 2:16-17

The dictionary defines the strange word abstemiousness" (Temperance) as being sparing or moderate in eating and drinking. We have all heard the motto, "Moderation in all things."

Usually it is understood that all "good things" are what is referred to. Surely we cannot endorse the moderate use of heroin, moderation in adultery or being moderately disposed to negative attitudes like hate, bigotry or deceit. A precise definition of abstemiousness would be "moderation (avoiding extremes) in those things that are good, and avoiding or totally abstaining from those things that are harmful."

In the introductory scripture God gives us the principle of abstemiousness upon which the right to enjoy eternal life is based. Adam and Eve were created in the image of God and had no disposition toward selfish self-gratification and so would naturally practice self-control or temperance. They had no tendencies toward the extremes. They were to practice moderation in their free eating of every tree in the garden. But they were not to eat from one certain tree- the tree of the knowledge of good and evil.

God wanted them to experience only good. Satan suggested that they ought to find out what a little evil would be like, too. They distrusted God and ate of the forbidden fruit. They broke the health principle of abstemiousness and decided to go beyond the moderate use of those things that are good and also throw in a little of the bad. Their disregard caused a change to take place in their very natures. Once giving in to a selfish desire, they had now opened the floodgate of intemperance and eventual death. God had warned them, "In the day that thou eatest thereof thou shalt surely die."

If God in His great love and mercy had not intervened, their situation would have been hopeless. God had a plan already in store just in case such an emergency should arise. This plan to save not only Adam and Eve from eternal death, but also all their descendants as well, is the main theme of the

172

entire Bible. It is God's way to restore to the human race perfect self-control, just as Adam and Eve had in the beginning. That way is Jesus Christ, the Son of God. "For God so loved the world, that he gave his only begotten Son, that whosoever believeth in him should not perish, but have everlasting life." John 3:16. "And this is the record, that God bath given to us eternal life, and this life is in his Son. He that hath the Son bath life; and he that bath not the Son of God bath not life." 1 John 5:11-12. The evidence that a person has received the Spirit of God in Christ is described in Galatians 5:22-23, "But the fruit of the Spirit is love, joy, peace, longsuffering, gentleness, goodness, faith, meekness, temperance: against such there is no law."

We can summarize what has been said up to this point as follows:

1. Abstemiousness is the moderate use of those things that are good, while abstaining from those things that are harmful.

2. This abstention requires self-control or temperance.

3. Temperance is a gift from God that comes to us only as we receive Christ.

Temperance, then, is required in order to build a lifestyle that is in balance physically, mentally,

socially, and spiritually. After all, without self-control we could not put into practice the

knowledge that we have. Unless we have the power to carry out all our good intentions, they are not of much use.

Once we have the power of God working in us, we can practice moderation in those things that are good. We will avoid extremes-the "over/unders."

Overeating leads to stomach-upset and/or obesity. Under-eating leads to malnutrition or starvation.

174

Overwork leads to exhaustion or injury. Under-work leads to atrophy and weakness.

Over-rest leads to weakness and laziness. Under-rest breeds mental confusion and exhaustion.

We also need a balanced intake of air, water, and sunlight--not too much and not too little.

Abstemiousness should regulate not only our physical health habits, but the mental and social aspects of life as well. Too much reading, too much talking, too much thinking, too much entertainment, too much sports, too much television, materialism, and fashion-all of these things, if not properly regulated, can overtax the mental powers and even lead to physical breakdown somewhere in the body. It could even be said that they are, in a way, intoxicating when carried to excess. We're familiar with the expressions "glued to the TV" or "sports fan" (short for fanatic). These examples serve to illustrate how one's entire life can be-come unbalanced and the mind somewhat intoxicated or warped by overstimulation. The Bible teaches us, Philippians 4:8. "Whatsoever things are true, whatsoever things are honest, whatsoever things are just, whatsoever things are pure, whatsoever things are lovely, whatsoever things &e of good report; if there be any virtue, and if there be any praise, think on these things."

This antidote would certainly be effective for many of society's mental and social ills.

Alcohol, tobacco, and caffeine, as commonly used (excluding rare medicinal usages), do no good whatsoever and have been proved to trigger many harmful side effects, depending on the pattern of use. Each one has its place to some degree in the lineup of prime suspects contributing to the epidemic of the degenerative disease-- atherosclerosis, osteoporosis, cancer, hypertension, diabetes, obesity, and so on. They also play a role in violent behavior, accidents and fires. There is almost always

176

some degree of dependence involved in their use. Aside from the physical harm done, this dependency is detrimental mentally and socially, as the user is subconsciously conditioned to use them as crutches. The development of important problem-solving skills and everyday coping skills is retarded to the extent that the chemical crutch is used as a substitute. All that the user need do to discover the extent of their dependency is to stop their use.

Illegal drugs should be rejected for the same reasons. They carry the additional drawback of moral guilt and possible civil punishment. Even over-the-counter prescript ion drugs should be avoided. They always carry side effects, many times do not work as they should, and usually there are safer alternative remedies that could be used instead.

Sometimes strong medications are the lesser of two evils, and in such cases their use is justified. Until something better is found, their use may be necessary.

John 15:5. "I am the vine, ye are the branches: he that abideth in me, and I in him, the same bringeth forth much fruit: for without me ye can do nothing."

It must be remembered that genuine self-control is a gift from God that we can receive only in Christ. Jesus said, We often in this life find ourselves at the end of our rope. But in God we have an infinite store of resources. So much so that the apostle Paul could say, Philippians 4:13 "I can do all things through Christ which strengtheneth me."

HOW TO OBTAIN DIVINE HELP OVER TOBACCO OR OTHER HARMFUL HABITS

1. Realize that you need help to be set free from tobacco (John 15:5; Jeremiah 33:3).

2. Know that God desires to provide this help to you (Isaiah 41:10).

3. Acknowledge your need and your willingness to come to God and fully cooperate with Him in causing a complete

178

change to happen in your life (Matthew 11:28-30). It is vital that you not live in a state of denial. Acknowledge to God, verbally, your condition and need. Ask Him to give to you a change of mind about tobacco or other habit. Tobacco or addiction is not to be your master (Matthew 23:10). This can only happen if you have a change of mind (heart).

Confess your guilt and ask for release from the guilt and power of tobacco (I John 1:9; Proverbs 28:13).

4. Ask for divine help to be set free from tobacco or other habit (Matthew 7:7, 8).

5. Choose to believe that God will fulfill His Word to give you perfect freedom over bad habits (Mark 9:22, 23).

6. Express trust in God and His promise to help you gain perfect freedom from tobacco or other problem (Luke 11:13).

7. Act on your belief by making a commitment to live a life of self-control

enabled by God's power (John 1:12). It is not enough to be sorry. You must actively turn away from your former lifestyle (I Corinthians 9:24- 27).

8. Spend time fixing the divine promises in your memory. These promises will bring power into your life when you are assailed by perverted cravings. This is the weapon that Jesus Himself used when He was tempted on appetite (Matthew 4:4).

9. Ask for help in every time of temptation (Luke 18:1, 7, 8; James 4:7-9). (God is not wearied by your continued requests for deliverance.)

10. Express your joy verbally; thank God for helping you to control your appetite (Philippians 4:4-7).

AIR

Pure fresh air is very important. That means good air with lots of oxygen. Walking in forests and nature is great. Do deep breathing exercises daily, in the morning. Even in winter have windows open a little and air rooms daily. Avoid smoke, chemicals, sprays and aerosols..

AND God said, Let there be a firmament in the midst of the waters, and let it divide the waters from the waters. And God made the firmament, and divided the waters which were under the firmament from the waters which were above the firmament: and it was so. And God called the firmament Heaven, And the evening and the morning were the second day." Genesis 1:6-8

And the LORD God formed man of the dust of the ground, and breathed into his nostrils the breath of life; and man became a living soul. Gen.2.7

The Most essential element to sustain life is oxygen.

• Without food you will die in a few weeks.

- Without water you will die in a few days.
- Without air you will die in a few minutes.

- Blood and cells are dependent upon oxygen.

Fresh air invigorates the vital organs and aids the system in ridding itself of accumulated impurities. Fresh air also brings life to the skin and has a decided influence on the mind.

Fresh air contains negative ions which help to immune system fight disease. The lack of fresh air causes specific problems such as fevers, colds, and lung diseases.

"The stomach, liver, lungs and brain are suffering for want of deep, full inspirations of air which would electrify the blood and impart to it a bright, lively color, and which alone can keep it pure, and give tone and vigor to every part of the living machinery." - - Ellen G. White, Testimonies Vol. 2, pp. 67-68

In the morning, step outside and breathe deeply; then expel all the air in your lungs. Repeat this about 3 or 4 times. Have fresh air ventilating in your home day and night. Exercise in the open air will promote good circulation. air is the free blessing of Heaven.

"In the matchless gift of His Son, God has encircled the whole world with an atmosphere of grace as real as the air which circulates around the globe. All who chose to breathe this life- giving atmosphere will live and grow up to the stature of men and women in Christ Jesus." --Ellen G. White, Steps to Christ, p. 68

The inside of the lung resembles a sponge. All of these tiny pockets (about 300 million) provide over seventy square yards of surface area for the exchange of gases in and out of the blood stream. An adult breathes about 16 times per minute, taking in about one pint of air per breath.

This intake adds up to about 2,000 gallons of air per day. During normal breathing this air travels at about 50 miles per hour, but during a sneeze or cough it can reach speeds of 750 miles per hour.

The maximum amount of air a person can inhale and exhale in one breath is called the vital capacity. A good vital capacity is related to a greater life expectancy. Several factors can affect a person's vital capacity: smoking, air pollution, posture, exercise, obesity, and shallow breathing.

For the person who smokes, the dangers are listed on the cigarette packages themselves. Lung cancer, emphysema, and carbon monoxide poisoning are among them. With every puff of smoke the air passageways narrow, making it more difficult to breathe. The cilia are paralyzed, thus preventing them from doing their job of cleansing the lungs. Mucus-clogged and irritated air passageways are ripe for emphysema and bronchitis. Carbon monoxide reduces the oxygen-carrying capacity of the blood. Nicotine constricts the blood vessels, elevates the blood pressure and heart rate, and irritates the heart itself.

In pregnant women these poisons cross the placenta and harm the fetus. Cancer-producing tars blacken the lungs. Marijuana smoke has many of the same health-damaging effects, plus some that are unique. Its active ingredient, THC, stays in the body longer than any other drug. With continued use it builds up in the fatty tissues, especially in the brain and in the testes and ovaries.

Cigarette smoke is also one of the main indoor-air pollutants. Those regularly exposed to second-hand smoke over an extended period of time are put at a significant risk for developing the same diseases and sharing some of the same physical impairments as the smoker. Small children, pregnant and lactating women, the elderly, and these with respiratory or heart diseases are the most vulnerable, and may not even be able to tolerate minimal exposure.

These persons are also the ones most likely to be affected by other types of indoor pollution.

Bacteria, molds, fungi, house mites, and other disease-producing organisms have a hard time multiplying in rooms that are kept well-aired and sunned. Make sure your ceiling, walls, and floor are adequately insulated to minimize as much unnecessary heat loss as possible. Energy conservation need not be at the expense of one's health. Also to ensure a supply of fresh air while sleeping in bed, open the windows in another room and keep your bedroom door open. Thus the fresh night air can get in without your being in a draft and getting chilled.

If you live in the city, the early morning hours usually have the cleanest air. It is also a good idea to take advantage of clear days by getting outdoors. The best way to escape air pollution is to live in the country. To give you an idea as to the potential differences in air quality, mid-Pacific ocean air contains about 15,000 particles per cubic inch of air as compared to 5,000,000 in big cities. In summary: "When the air is bad, try not to breathe it."

There is something else that makes fresh air fresh besides oxygen and the absence of pollutants, and that is the type of ionization in the air. Ions are tiny, electrified particles of matter. Fresh air may contain between 2-3 million ions in each breath, which is 5-10 times more than stale air. (Oxygen usually carries a negative charge and carbon dioxide a positive charge.) Aerospace research and experience has suggested that air ionization is in itself a health factor apart from the oxygen content alone.

We do not yet understand how it works, but numerous studies have associated negative ions, specifically negatively ionized oxygen, with several health benefits. These include an increased rate and quality of growth in plants and in animals, dilation of the air passageways and improvement in the cleansing action of the lungs, heart rate, blood pressure, and metabolic rate. Mentally, one can experience a sense of exhilaration, or become more relaxed and mildly tranquilized. Hay fever and asthma symptoms may improve. Tumor growth was slowed in laboratory animals. Rats learned twice as fast. Positively charged air, on the other hand, produced the opposite responses and tends to be associated with headaches, dizziness, nausea, and fatigue.

Negative ions are lost as they adhere to walls, fabric materials, and air-conditioning ducts; tobacco smoke, smog and crowds of people tend to use them up, too. Sunshine, living green trees, and the breakup of water droplets, as occurs around waterfalls and the ocean surf. add negative ions back into the air.

Now that we've cleared the air, there is one more thing to do, and that is to breathe properly.

Breathe in and out through the nose as much as possible. The nasal mucosa moisturizes, filters, and warms the air as it is breathed in. As it is breathed out some heat and moisture is returned to the membranes to affect the next breath.

Oxygen is the most crucial element for our survival. We can survive weeks without food, days without water; but only minutes without oxygen. Yet because of shallow breathing habits we can deny ourselves optimal levels of oxygen for better health. Early signs of insufficient oxygen are impaired judgment and memory, dulling of intellect, and a tendency to impatience and irritability.

Many people are forced to stoop or sit for much of the day. This usually makes for poor posture and causes many back problems. Maintaining good posture, taking stretch breaks often, and getting exercise whenever you can will help. Remember when walking, to visualize that string again supporting you from the top of your head and thus avoid walking with your neck thrust forward thus interfering with breathing. After all, even if your nose does get there first, nothing much will be done until the rest of you arrives.

A good aerobic exercise program combined with muscle toning and stretching exercises is necessary for good health besides being an aid to proper breathing and maintaining a strong set of lungs.

Tight clothing around the chest or abdomen makes proper breathing difficult, as does restrictive clothing that does not allow the free movement of the arms above the head. It is better for women to avoid the unhealthful fashion of tight bras and wear a camisole or undershirt instead.

Normal deep breathing aids digestion by massaging the abdominal organs. Blood is assisted in its return to the chest by the negative pressure that is developed with each deep breath. This pressure helps to reduce the chances of congestion headaches, the pooling of blood in the legs, and aids in the digestive process. Deep breathing gets more

190

oxygen into the blood with each breath, allowing the heart to slow down a little.

A good habit is to go outside in the fresh air and take 10~20 slow, deep, abdominal breaths after each meal and just before retiring for the night. And as we enjoy this time of relaxation, we can give thanks to our Creator God "that giveth breath unto the people." Remembering that "He giveth to all life, and breath, and all things." So, "let every thing that hath breath praise the LORD. Praise ye the LORD." Isaiah 42:5; Acts 17:25; Psalm 150:6

REST

Matthew 11.28-30 Come unto me, all ye that labour and are heavy laden, and I will give you rest. Take my yoke upon you, and learn of me; for I am meek and lowly in heart: and ye shall find rest unto your souls. For my yoke is easy, and my burden is light.

Genesis 2:2

"He rested on the seventh day from all His work which He had made."

• The greatest remedy for being tired is SLEEP.

• The body requires plenty of rest to heal.

• Sleep is the greatest rejuvenator; it restores strength to muscles, nerves, and brain.

• During sleep the body repairs, reenergizes, and prepares for renewed activity.

• One hour of sleep before midnight is equal to 2 hours of sleep after midnight.

During a day of work and activity, toxins build up in our system which cannot immediately be thrown off. These toxins product fatigue--that well-known weariness at the end of the day. Sleep gives the body time to expel wastes and to make repairs.

"The stomach, when we lie down to rest, should have its work done, that it may enjoy rest, as well as other portions of the body. The work of digestion should not be carried on through any period of the sleeping hours." -- Ellen G. White, Healthful Living, p. 84

Rest is not synonymous with sleep. Four types of rest are:

• **Physical Rest** -- sitting, lying down, or relaxing. Not eating late at night or before bed.

• **Sensory Rest** -- quietness and refraining from using the eyes.
• **Emotional Rest** -- a withdrawing from the ups and downs caused by person interaction.

• **Mental Rest** -- a detaching of the mind from all intellectual demands or activity.

Your Prescription: First, get the sleep your body needs, 8 hours a day and several hours before midnight. Second, do not neglect that important rest we need, such as taking morning walks, sitting in a garden or other pleasant surroundings, or by a mountain side, looking at a forest or lake, going to the ocean, or reading the Scriptures.

"A life in Christ is a life of restfulness. There may be no ecstasy of feeling, but there should be an abiding peaceful trust. Your hope is not in yourself; it is in Christ. Your weakness is united to His strength, your ignorance to His wisdom, your frailty to His enduring might....Let the mind dwell upon His love, upon the beauty, the perfection of His character." -- Ellen G. White, Steps to Christ, p.70

Get adequate restful sleep. An early, light supper, well before bedtime and no eating before bed will help. A relaxing warm bath may help you unwind; avoid stressful and stimulating activities before bedtime. Regular times for going to bed and rising will also help. The best time to go to bed is between 8 and 10 PM. This sounds strange, because in our culture, it almost seems in bad taste to sleep. 100 years ago the average person got 9 or more hours sleep. Now it is more like 4 or 5. Exercise during the day also helps set the stage for restful sleep. Avoid using drugs for sleep as these are harmful and sleep thus attained is of little benefit to your body. Lack of restful sleep is for many the root of the 'enervation' that brings disease. For healing and cleansing to occur much rest and sleep is needed as these actions are done only while asleep.

Those who have trouble falling asleep can try a little hops, chamomile or catnip tea before bedtime. Slow, deep breathing or soaking in a neutral bath with a cup of Epsom salts added for ten minutes may help. Blot the skin dry and move slowly and quietly off to bed.

TRUST IN GOD

Proverbs 3.5-8

Trust in the LORD with all thine heart; and lean not unto thine own understanding. In all thy ways acknowledge him, and he shall direct thy paths. Be not wise in thine own eyes: fear the LORD, and depart from evil. It shall be health to thy navel, and marrow to thy bones.

"And the rib, which the Lord God had taken from man, made He a woman, and brought her unto the man." Genesis 2:22

Who is the Great Physician?

Psalm 103:3 "Who forgiveth all thine iniquities; who healeth all thy diseases;"

Luke 4:40 "Now when the sun was setting, all they that had any sick with divers diseases brought them unto him; and he laid his hands on every one of them, and healed them".

From whom does all healing come?

Exodus 15:26"If thou will diligently hearken to the voice of the Lord thy God, and will do that which is right in His sight, and will give ear to His commandment, and keep His statutes, I will put none of the diseases upon thee, which I have brought upon the Egyptians: for I am the Lord that healeth thee."

Proverbs 3:5, 8"Trust in the Lord with all thine heart, and lean not unto thine own understanding....it shall be health to thy navel, and marrow to thy bones."
What is His desire for your life?

3 John 2 "Beloved, I wish above all things that you may prosper and be in health, even as your soul prospereth."

Deuteronomy 7:11, 15 "Thou shalt therefore keep the commandments...which I command thee this day, to do them...and the Lord will take away all sickness and will put none of the evil diseases of Egypt...upon thee."

Does He want our complete restoration?

1 Thessalonians 5:23 "And the very God of peace sanctify you wholly; and I pray God your whole spirit and soul and body be preserved blameless unto the coming of our Lord Jesus Christ."

Does a lack of trust create a negative influence?

Hebrews 11:6 "But without faith it is impossible to please Him: for he that cometh to God must believe that He is, and the He is a rewarded of them that diligently seek Him."

Proverbs 17:22 "A merry heart doeth good like a medicine: but a broken spirit drieth the bones."

Proverbs 14:30 "A sound heart is the life of the flesh; but envy the rottenness of the bones."

Remember, worry, stress, and depression bring decay, disease, and death. The immune system is strengthened by trusting God.

The foundation of all health is in the acceptance of the blessings which the Creator has provided for us. Foremost of these is the privilege we have of choosing our Saviour to be our Guide as well as our Great Physician. In fact, the divine purpose of our physical healing is to make us more inclined to accept the spiritual healing Christ longs to perform upon our hearts.

There is an inexpressible peace that comes to one who has learned to trust in God and to lay all things in His hands. In Matthew 11:28 Jesus says, "Come unto Me...and I will give your rest."

Rest from sorrow, rest from fear, and rest from insecurity. But first we must come to Him as our Great Physician. We must trust Him before we can understand and practice His profession or reveal His wisdom and love.

The let us resign ourselves to do His will, and endeavor faithfully to follow every instruction He gives for when we come to God, we must be willing to acknowledge and accept His ways as best for us, and follow them, regardless of our own personal preference and prejudices. There may be times when we may not discern His wisdom in certain events, but it is on these occasions that we especially honor Him by our faith. By being obedient to Him in those things which He askes of us--be it in the physical or spiritual realm--we shall discover that He is guiding us on our way to complete healing.

"Keep your wants, your joys, your sorrows, your cares, and your fears before God.... 'The Lord is very pitiful and of tender mercy.' James 5:11. His heart of love is touched by our sorrows and even by our utterances of them.... Nothing that in any way concerns our peace is too small for Him to notice. There is no chapter in our experience too dark for Him to read; there is no perplexity too difficult for Him to unravel. No calamity can befall the least of His children, no anxiety harass the soul, no joy, cheer, no sincere prayer escape the lips, of which our heavenly Father is unobservant, or in which He takes no immediate interest. 'He healeth the broken in heart and bindeth up their wounds.' Psalm 147:3." -- Ellen G. White, Steps to Christ, p. 100

"Through nature and revelation, through His providence, and by the influence of His Holy Spirit, God speaks to us. But these are not enough; we need also to pour out our hearts to Him. In order to have spiritual life and energy, we must have actual intercourse with our heavenly Father...

"Prayer is the opening of the heart to God as to a friend.... Prayer does not bring God down to us, but brings us up to Him.

"He [Jesus] found comfort and joy in communion with His Father. And if the Saviour of men, the Son of God, felt the need of prayer, how much more should feeble, sinful mortals feel the necessity of fervent, constant prayer." Ibid, pp. 64, 65

Revelation 3:20 "Behold, I stand at the door and knock: if any man hear My voice, and open the door, I will come in and sup with him, and he with Me."

May we never forget:

Deuteronomy 7:24 "And the Lord commanded us to do all these statutes, to fear the Lord our God, for our good always, that He might preserve us alive, as it is at this day."

Courtesy of Present Truth

Pure fresh air is very important. That means good air with lots of oxygen. Walking in forests and nature is great. Do deep breathing exercises daily, in the morning. Even in winter have windows open a little and air rooms daily. Avoid smoke, chemicals, sprays and aerosols..

AND God said, Let there be a firmament in the midst of the waters, and let it divide the waters from the waters. And God made the firmament, and divided the waters which were under the firmament from the waters which were above the firmament: and it was so. And God called the firmament Heaven, And the evening and the morning were the second day." Genesis 1:6-8

About the Author

Leola Sanders Huey is 89 years old. She was born during the Depression, when the only media was the radio, Victrola record and party line; if you could afford any one of those.

The most entertainment in Leola's home was storytelling by her mother about her life. Life stories were mostly told among family and friends to their children. Unfortunately, the media has taken the place of storytelling. Leola decided to become a storyteller to keep the stories alive for the younger generations. She also writes life stories about her time and age. This is the third book that she has written. She published her first book at the age of 82 and has two more books to write in the future. She never gave up her dream of wanting to become a writer. She is proof that you can never be too old to fulfill your dreams and be used by God.

About the Author

www.ingramcontent.com/pod-product-compliance
Lightning Source LLC
Chambersburg PA
CBHW072003060426
42446CB00042B/1514